LET'S GOLF!

DRIVING HOME TIPS OF THE GAME

James D. George
Brigham Young University

PEARSON

Benjamin
Cummings

San Francisco   Boston   New York
Cape Town   Hong Kong   London   Madrid   Mexico City
Montreal   Munich   Paris   Singapore   Sydney   Tokyo   Toronto

PUBLISHER: Daryl Fox
ACQUISITIONS EDITOR:
  Deirdre McGill
PROJECT EDITOR: Susan Malloy
MARKETING MANAGER:
  Sandra Lindelof
DEVELOPMENT MANAGER:
  Claire Brassert
PRODUCTION EDITOR:
  Steven Anderson
PROJECT COORDINATION
  AND COMPOSITION: The Left
  Coast Group

COPY EDITOR: Gary Morris
PROOFREADER: Martha Ghent
TEXT DESIGNER: The Left
  Coast Group
COVER DESIGNER: Yvo Riezebos
MANUFACTURING BUYER:
  Stacey Weinberger
COVER PRINTER: Phoenix Color
PRINTER: Malloy Lithographing,
  Inc.
COVER PHOTO: Photodisc

ISBN 0-8053-2835-1

Copyright © 2004 by Pearson Education, Inc., publishing as Pearson Benjamin Cummings, San Francisco, CA 94111. All rights reserved. Printed in the United States of America. This publication is protected by Copyright and permission should be obtained from the publisher prior to any prohibited reproduction, storage in a retrieval system, or transmission in any form or by any means, electronic, mechanical, photocopying, recording, or likewise. For information regarding permission(s), write to: Pearson Education, Inc., Rights and Permissions Department.

PEARSON

*To my older brother Richard,
who got me hooked on this great game.*

To my Uncle Reynold, who gave me my first clubs.

*To my friend and mentor Garth Fisher,
who continues to teach me so much about the game.*

*To the many golfers I've taught over the years,
who helped me become a better teacher and
encouraged me to publish this book.*

*And finally, to my wonderfully talented wife,
Shaunna, whose love and support
make everything possible.*

Acknowledgments

Many thanks to the people at BYU who helped me develop the initial drafts of this book—the editors Shaunna George, Annie Green, Brittany Candrian, Maggie Shibla, Don Norton, and the BYU faculty editing service; the photographers Ron Hager, Ben Seager, Brent Feland, and Mark Philbrick; and the models (golfers) Tadd Cox, Stephanie Belnap, Jose Garrido, and Mike George.

Also, many thanks to the people at Benjamin Cummings (Deirdre McGill, Michelle Cadden, Susan Malloy, Diane Southworth, and team), The Left Coast Group, Gary Morris, Martha Ghent, and the outside book reviewers (Brent Feland, Brigham Young University; A. Garth Fisher, Brigham Young University; Randall Goble, Kennesaw State University; Kyle Savage, University of Maryland; Craig Snyder, Nike Golf Camps; Allys Swanson, College of St. Catherine; Robert Wiegand, West Virginia University) who did a splendid job in taking this book to the next level. The experience, from start to finish, has been a slam-dunk hole-in-one from 200 yards!

Contents

"MUST-KNOW" SKILLS

RULES, LOGS, AND MORE

This guidebook was fun to write, and I hope it's fun for you to read. My goal from the very beginning was to put together the very best golf book possible. I've reached this goal if, as you read it, you say to yourself:

- "This book is so clear and easy to understand."
- "It's great to know how to swing and what to do when I practice and play."
- "This book is so organized and upbeat. It makes golf fun!"
- "The pictures in this book make it easy to see what's going on."
- "It answers all of my big questions about the game."
- "I'm impressed with the practice activities in each section of the book."
- "Golf is my favorite sport!"
- "I love this book!"

I've given hundreds and hundreds of lessons over the nearly 20 years I've taught golf. During this time I've figured out what beginning and intermediate golfers need to know to improve their game. I've also read almost every golf book ever written and studied piles of instructional articles from the monthly golf magazines. It's incredible how much there is to know about this game (and no book can tell it all), but I believe you'll be happy with what you learn if you hunker down and study this guidebook carefully.

The other day I had to smile. I was walking across our campus and overheard a bright young lady raving to her friend about how much she loves golf. She went on and on! With the deepest enthusiasm you can imagine, she talked about how much she loves being out on the course, golfing with her friends, enjoying the outdoors, learning how to swing, and so on. I hope that you will have a similar experience. Golf truly is one of the greatest games ever invented. So grab your clubs and get out there and enjoy it in every way!

GETTING STARTED . . .

⛳ 1 LET'S GOLF!

1

LET'S GOLF!

The best instruction is short, sweet, and always to the point.

—*GOLF MAGAZINE*, 2001

Hey, I've Got a Question!

1. "I'm a beginning golfer. Can you help me understand all this golf lingo?" You might be a little confused for a while, but don't worry! You'll catch on quickly to this new "golf talk." To help you get started, here's a rundown

know.

"Let's play a *round* of golf next Friday."

Playing a round of golf means to play 9 or 18 holes. It's been called a "round" ever since golf was first invented because you begin and end at about the same place on the course. If you look at the backside of any scorecard, you'll probably find a simple map of the course. Notice how the first hole goes away from the clubhouse and the last one loops back. This is how every golf course is set up.

"I'm going to play from the *front tees*."

Not everyone starts each hole at the same place. You can choose to play from the set of tee markers (or tee box) that are best for you. As a beginner, it's smart to go as far forward as possible and play from the front tee box (often red or gold). This shortens the course and makes it a lot easier to play. A little farther back, you'll find the white or blue

---

⟡ QUICK TIP ⟡

Whenever you play a round, always pick up a scorecard and pencil in the Pro Shop (they're free). If you're playing a course for the first time, refer to the scorecard map so you don't accidentally play the wrong hole. The map also shows the basic shape of each hole so you'll know if the hole is straight or bends (doglegs) to the left or right. Some maps also point out the various trouble spots to stay away from, such as lakes and rivers, out-of-bound areas, sand bunkers, and other problem areas.

middle tee markers. These are geared for the intermediate player and offer a bit more of a challenge. When you're ready for the ultimate challenge, you can move back with the pros and hit from the back tee markers (usually blue or black).

> ◆ **QUICK TIP** ◆
>
> Look over any scorecard and you'll find the exact length of each hole (depending on which tee box you play from) and the total distance of all 18 holes. Added together, most regulation 18-hole golf courses range anywhere from 6,000 to 7,200 yards. You might not realize it, but playing golf is a great form of exercise, especially when you walk the course and carry your own bag. By the end of 9 holes, you will have walked well over three miles and burned lots of energy along the way.

shot?"

The rules of golf allow you to tee up your ball (in the tee box) when hitting your first shot on each hole. This is a good idea because it keeps any extra grass out of the way and makes the shot easier to

hit. To tee up your ball, first find a level area between the tee markers (but not in front of them). Place your ball in the palm of your hand, with the tee between your first and second fingers. Using the weight of the ball, push the tee down in the turf until it's at the right height.

◄● How high you tee your ball depends on the club you're using. For your driver (1-wood), set the tee high enough so that about half your ball is below the top surface of the wood and the other half is above it. For any iron or fairway wood (3- or 5-wood), use a broken or full tee and set the tee height so the ball is about level with the top of the grass. Experiment until you find a tee height that is perfect for the club you are using and your particular swing.

5

"Can I make the *tee-time* this week?"

When you want to play golf with your friends, ask a member of your group to phone the course a day or so beforehand and set up a tee-time. This is a smart way to go because you know you'll be paired with your friends and reserve the time you want. To make a tee-time, call the pro shop and tell the golf course staff member (or "starter"):

1. When you would like to play.
2. The number of players in your group.
3. The number of holes you plan to play (9 or 18).

Most tee-times run every 8 minutes, so don't be surprised if you're given a time like 10:08 A.M. or 3:32 P.M. Once you've got a tee-time, call your friends so they'll know when to be at the course. As a rule, try to get to the course at least 30 minutes early so you can have plenty of time to check in at the pro shop, pay your greens fees, hit some practice shots, and get ready to go out and play.

If for some reason you can't get a tee-time, most courses will let you try to "walk on." The plan here is to check in at the pro shop right when you get to the course and ask to have your name put on a waiting list.

◆ QUICK TIP ◆

Not all courses have the same tee-time policies. For instance, some courses take tee-times only the day before, while others schedule them a week in advance. If you're not sure, check with the course beforehand so you'll have the best chance of getting the tee-times you want.

When a spot opens up, the starter will invite you to go to either the 1st or 10th hole and join other players. The wait normally isn't that bad, especially if the course isn't too busy or you're playing as a single and don't mind being paired with another group.

"The starter in the pro shop said we should play as a *foursome*."

Most of the time the starter will ask you to play in groups of two, three, or four (on the golf course these are called twosomes, threesomes, and foursomes). If the course isn't too busy, you can also play as a single if you'd like. Keep in mind, though, that you'll need special permission from the pro shop to play in a group of five (a fivesome).

Most golfers enjoy being paired with other players. It's fun to socialize, watch other swings, talk about the latest PGA tournament, compare golf equipment, and share golf stories. As a beginning golfer, you may be too intimidated to play with other golfers you don't know, but soon you'll look forward to meeting new players.

"You hit the *fairway*. Nice shot!"

Each hole has three parts: the teeing area, the fairway, and the putting green. As mentioned before, the tee box is the starting point of each hole. The fairway runs from the tee box to the green and is usually the shortest route to the green. It's also the safest approach since the fairway grass is cut short, making your next shot a lot easier to hit. As you know, the green is where you'll find the cup (or hole). A long fiberglass pole with a flag on the top (the flagstick) marks the cup, so you can easily see where it is located when you're hitting from the tee or the fairway.

"I think your shot is either in the *rough* or in the *hazard*."

If your shot veers off to the left or to the right, it may stop in the rough, which is the extra-long grass on either side of the fairway. This is something every golfer tries to avoid since the long grass usually grabs your club during the swing and makes it hard to contact the ball solidly. Plus, any time you're off the fairway you might find yourself behind a big tree or two, making it impossible to hit your ball directly toward the green.

Another problem with missing the fairway is that your ball might fly into a hazard. These include sand bunkers and water hazards. A sand bunker (or sand trap) is a part of the course where the turf has been removed and replaced with sand. With a good swing, it's possible to get out of a bunker without it hurting your score, but more often than not, any shot that runs off the fairway may cost you a stroke or two by the time you finish the hole. If your ball happens to disappear in a water hazard (lake or river), you'll need to add a penalty stroke to your score to get your ball back into play. (See Hole 17 for more information on the rules.)

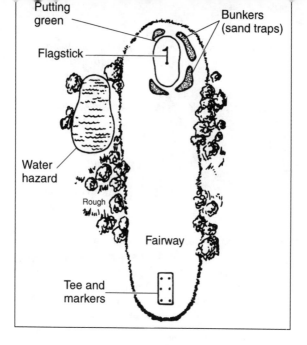

"From that *yardage marker,* I'm 100 yards from the cup."
Most courses have yardage markers along the fairway, making it easy to know how many more yards it will take to reach the green. For example, you might see small number plates glued to the top of various sprinkler heads telling

 you the exact distance to the middle of the green. It's also common to see a small sign, pole, or bush set off to the side of the fairway that's exactly 150 yards from the front or middle of the green. Knowing the exact yardage to the green helps you pick the right club for the upcoming shot.

"My shot *sliced* off into the rough."

You'll hear golfers use all kinds of words to describe the trajectory and direction of their shots. "I hooked that one." "I'm going to draw this shot around the corner." "I hit that ball thin." The list goes on and on, but here's a brief summary of some of the most common terms you need to know about.

A shot that . . .

- Curves to the right is a slice
- Curves to the left is a hook
- Curves *slightly* to the right is a fade
- Curves *slightly* to the left is a draw
- Flies straight but goes to the right of the target is a push
- Flies straight but goes to the left of the target is a pull

called a line drive, thin, or sculled shot
- Pops up and flies really high is a sky

"Wow, I finally scored a *par*!"

Each hole has a par, which is the number of strokes a very good golfer takes to sink his or her ball into the cup. Generally speaking, the longer the hole, the higher the par. The shortest holes (85 to 200 yards) are par threes, the medium-length holes (250 to 425 yards) are par fours, and the longest holes (425 to 550 yards) are par fives.

On a regulation golf course, the first nine holes (the front nine) often have two 3-par holes, five 4-par holes, and two 5-par holes. If you score a par on every hole, your total strokes add up to 36. The par on the second 9 holes (or back 9) is usually the same, so a score of 72 is "even par" when you play the entire 18 holes.

Only the very best players can shoot even par. To do this, they try to reach each green in "regulation." This means to hit every 3-par green in one shot, every 4-par green in two shots, and every 5-par green in three shots. Once the ball is on the green, the goal is to take no more than two putts to hole the ball. If this happens on every hole, it's called an even par score for the round. Of course, it's not easy to hit every green in regulation and two-putt every green, but some players can do it.

Most golfers are happy to finish one stroke over par on each hole. This score is called a "bogie." Scoring two strokes over par is called a "double bogie," three over par is called a "triple bogie," and so on. Some golfers also use the term "double par," which means to take twice as many strokes as par (or a six on a 3-par), or "snowman," which means to score an eight on any hole.

One stroke less than par is called a "birdie" (a three on a 4-par). An even better score is an "eagle," which is two under par (a three on a 5-par or a two on a 4-par). The rare "double-eagle" (also known as an "albatross") is a score of two on a 5-par. The most exciting shot of all is the "ace" (hole-in-one), where the player takes only one shot to hole his or her ball.

At the end of the round, golfers talk about their score in a few different ways. For example, a score of "10 over" means the player took 82 strokes on a par-72 course. Playing "bogie golf" is another way of saying that the average score on each hole was 1 over par (which equals 18 over par or 90 strokes on a par-72 course). Shooting 3 under par (a 69) means that the player had three birdies and averaged par on the other holes.

It's also interesting to know that the very best 18-hole score in a professional tournament is 59, or 13 under par. Al Geiberger, in 1972, was the first to do it while playing on the Men's PGA tour. (Recently, Chip Beck and David Duval also did it.) Annika Sorenstam,

---

♪ WORDS TO KNOW

Par: The number of strokes an excellent golfer takes to complete a hole.

Bogie: A score of one stroke above par on a hole.

Double bogie: A score of two strokes above par on a hole.

Birdie: A score of one stroke less than par on a hole.

Eagle: A score of two strokes less than par on a hole.

Date	Event
1353	Reference to Chole, an antecedent of golf
1552	First evidence of golf at St. Andrews, Scotland
1618	Feathery ball invented
1754	Royal and ancient golf club of St. Andrews founded
1860	British Open Championship initiated
1895	United States Open initiated
1905	First dimple-pattern golf ball patented
1916	PGA of America founded
1933	Augusta National Golf Club opens (home of the Masters)
1945	Byron Nelson wins 18 tournaments in a single calendar year
1962	Jack Nicklaus wins first professional tournament: the U.S. Open
1972	Al Geiberger shoots 59
1979	Taylor Made introduces first metal woods
1996	Tiger Woods wins his third consecutive U.S. Amateur title
2000	Tiger Woods wins three Majors in single season
2001	Annika Sorenstam shoots 59

ADAPTED FROM: *GOLFONLINE,* 2002

in 2001, was the first woman to get this score while playing on the Ladies PGA tour. This is an amazing accomplishment because it means that these players scored a birdie on nearly every hole!

"That course was too tough! Next time I'm going to an *executive course*."

If you play a course that's too challenging, even from the front tees, it's best to find a little easier course. Most beginners opt for what's called an executive course. These are very short courses with mostly par threes. The total distance of a 9-hole executive course can be no more than 1,500 yards (compared to up to 3,500 yards for a regulation course). Once you build your skills and confidence, you can easily switch back to the longer, more challenging courses.

"I've heard golfers talk about their *handicap*. What is this about?"

In general, your average score compared to par is the basis for your handicap. The lower the handicap, the better you can play. Depending on how hard the course is, your handicap roughly equals the number of strokes over par you shoot on 18 holes. For example, if you get down to a zero handicap (a "scratch golfer"), it means you can score close to even par on 18 holes. If you have an 18-handicap, it tells other golfers you play around bogie golf (or 90 on a par-72 course). For men, handicaps run from 0 to 36; for women, from 0 to 40. The United States Golf Association (USGA) figures that about 20 percent of male golfers have a single digit handicap and about 70 percent are 18 or better. Among female players, fewer than 5 percent are at 10 or better and about 60 percent have a handicap less than 30.

If you're interested in getting a handicap for yourself, go to your local course and ask the pro for details. It involves playing the required number of holes, posting your scores, and paying a small fee. Your golf pro will e-mail your info to your state golf office and your official USGA handicap will be computed.

To figure your handicap, officials enter three things into a formula: your golf scores, the course rating, and the course slope. When the results come back, the pro will give you a small card with your handicap on it (to keep in your wallet or golf bag) or just have you look up your handicap on the pro shop computer.

Most golfers get a handicap so they can play in local leagues or tournaments. If you decide to enter a tournament, you'll be placed in a division or "flight" based on your handicap. Common flights include the Championship Flight (0 to 6 handicap), First Flight (7–12 handicap), Second Flight (13–18 handicap), and Third Flight (over 18 handicap). At the end of the tournament, prize money (good for pro shop merchandise) is awarded to

---

⛳ WORDS TO KNOW

Course rating: The score a scratch golfer shoots on a course under normal course and weather conditions. Ratings run from 66 to 74, depending on the difficulty of the course (see scorecard for course rating info).

Course slope: A number showing how hard a course is for the average golfer. Slopes run from 55 to 155 (a higher number means a more challenging course; see scorecard for course slope info).

the top players in each flight based on gross and net scores. The gross score is simply the total stroke score without any adjustments. The net score is the gross score minus the player's handicap.

Because about half of tournament prizes come from net scores, the USGA assumes that every player will establish a legitimate handicap based on honest scores. However, since it can't police every round of golf, the honor system applies when it comes to tournament play. Sometimes there's a golfer in the mix who has a bogus handicap (they're called "sandbaggers"), but for the most part, golfers take the high road and do it right. If there is a concern, the USGA relies on two checkpoints to fix the problem. First, it asks golfers to post accurate scores in the pro shop after each round of golf. All scores are then open to the public so fellow players have the opportunity to review and correct inflated scores that may be turned in. Second, each course has a handicap committee that carefully looks over tournament scores and has the authority to lower a handicap if a golfer is playing well beyond his or her expected ability.

There is one other place you'll see the word handicap. On the scorecard of every regulation 9- or 18-hole course, each hole is assigned a handicap based on how hard it plays. The hardest hole is ranked 1, the second hardest is ranked 2, and so on all the way up to 18. Knowing this comes in handy when you play a course for the first time and wonder which holes offer the biggest challenge.

need?" Every golfer needs golf tees, golf balls, a golf bag, and clubs. A beginning golf set usually includes seven clubs: the 4-, 6-, and 8-irons; a pitching wedge; 1- and 5-woods; and a putter. A full set usually includes 14 clubs: the

3-, 4-, 5-, 6-, 7-, 8-, 9-irons; a pitching wedge; a lob wedge; a sand wedge; the 1-, 3-, and 5-woods; and a putter. Depending on how serious you are about the game, you might also want to get a golf glove and golf shoes with soft spikes.

> ## ◆● QUICK TIP ◆●
>
> Did you know some golf courses (usually private country clubs) enforce a dress code? Here's an example taken straight from a scorecard:
>
> **Dress Code:** *All shirts must have a collar, no denim, no cut-offs, golf shoes with soft spikes only. NO EXCEPTIONS.*
>
> But don't worry; most public courses are pretty easygoing and let you wear tee shirts, shorts, and tennis shoes. If you're not sure, call the course and ask for details. This way you won't be surprised when you get to the course.

3. **"There are lots of different golf shots, right? Can you tell me the main difference between each one?"** There are six different shots you need to know about.

Drive

This is the longest shot in golf (at least that's the goal) and is the first shot taken from the tee box on the long par fours and fives. Its purpose? To drive the ball far enough down the fairway so you can hit your next shot to the green. To do this, most players use a "driver" or 1-wood, although you don't

have to. The driver is actually the hardest club to hit straight with, so some players go with a 3-wood or an iron off the tee until their skills improve.

Approach Shot

The goal of an approach shot is to hit your ball on the green or to advance it down the fairway so your next shot can reach the green. It's usually hit with irons or fairway woods depending on the distance you need. In order to hit a good approach shot, you'll need to know the exact distance to the green, pick the right club, and take a good swing.

Chip

This is a short "bump-and-run" shot hit from right next to the green. If done right, a chip flies low for the first few yards and then rolls the rest of the way to the hole. It's usually hit with one of the short irons (7-, 8-, or 9-iron or pitching wedge). (Hole 6 outlines how to hit a chip shot.)

Pitch

This is a high-flying, quick-stopping approach shot that flies most of the way to the hole and rolls only a short distance. A pitch can be taken anywhere from just off the green to as far away as 100 yards from the flag. It's hit with a pitching, lob, or sand wedge, depending on how far the ball is from the hole. (Hole 7 gives a rundown of helpful tips and techniques.)

Sand Shot

If your shot strays a little off line, your ball might find the "beach"—one of those dreaded sand traps placed next to the green (a greenside bunker) or alongside the fairway (a fairway bunker). Although they're quite intimidating for the beginning golfer, sand traps really aren't that tough to handle when you know what to do. (Hole 13 shows you how to play from the sand.)

Putt

The putt is the easiest shot in golf, right? Think again! Rolling a 1.68-inch ball across the green into a 4.25-inch-wide hole might not look that hard, but it is! To sink your putts you've got to consider several things: the distance to the hole, the slope of the terrain, the length of the grass, and even the wind. After you figure this out, you've got to step up, get in the

right stance, take dead aim, make a good stroke, and hit your ball right on target. It's a fun and never-ending challenge! (Hole 8 provides the nuts and bolts on how to putt.)

shot?" It's not that easy to choose the right club, especially when you have 14 to choose from. If you pick the wrong one, your ball may end up well short of your target or fly way over it. After you put in plenty of practice, you'll come to know exactly how far each one of your clubs can hit the ball. At that point you will be able to stand on the third hole, have 120 yards to the green, and know that a good 9-iron shot will do the trick. Or, if you need to hit short of a river 195 yards away from the tee box, you'll know a nice 6-iron shot will keep you out of trouble. Here's a distance guide on how far the better players of the game hit each club:

IRONS (YARDS)		WOODS (YARDS)	
Sand wedge	80–120	5-wood	190–200
Pitching wedge	120–130	3-wood	215–225
9-iron	130–140	1-wood	240–280+
8-iron	140–150		
7-iron	150–160		
6-iron	160–170		
5-iron	170–180		
4-iron	180–190		
3-iron	190–200		
2-iron	200–210		

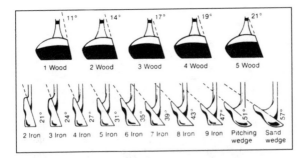

5. **"I've heard there are lots of little 'social graces' to follow when I'm out on the course. Is this true?"** Yes! In fact, here's a brief summary of what the USGA wants you to know about courtesy on the course (www.usga.org):

"Who's up? When is it my turn?"

When you get to the first tee, you and your playing partners can hit in any order. On the rest of the tee shots, take your turn based on how well you did on the previous hole. For example, the player with the lowest score has the "honor" to go first; the player with the second-to-lowest score goes next; and so on. If two or more players happen to tie, tee off in the same order as the previous hole.

from the hole is the next to play. As you make your way to the green, be ready to play when it's your turn. Once you reach the green, the player farthest from the hole putts first. If your putt happens to stop close to the hole, go ahead and tap in to save time and keep things mov-

ing (as you do this, just be careful not to step on the green where another player is planning to putt).

"Quiet please!"

Golf takes a lot of concentration, so it's important not to bother other players as they line up their shot or make a stroke. Use good manners: don't move, talk, jingle keys or coins, or stand close to or directly behind the ball or the hole when another player is preparing to play or taking his or her shot. Always be aware of what's going on around you. Treat other golfers as you would like to be treated!

"Replace your divots!"

During a good iron swing, your club should hit the ball first and then cut through the top layer of turf. The grass and soil that flies forward is called a "divot." It's perfectly fine to watch your shot (and hopefully enjoy it!), but don't go forward until you repair the divot. There are two ways to do this: 1) Retrieve the grass and carefully put it back in the divot mark, and then gently step down on it. 2) If a mixture

of sand and grass seed is provided (in a small box alongside the teeing area or in your golf cart), pour some over the divot mark and smooth it out. Doing this makes a big difference and helps the grass grow back much sooner.

"Rake the trap!"

After any shot from a sand bunker, you'll need to do some cleanup work. Use the rake that's provided alongside the bunker. Walk slowly backwards and smooth out all footprints and other rough spots.

"Tend the flag!"

When you're putting from the green, the USGA doesn't want you to use the flagstick as a backstop. In fact, it's a two-stroke penalty if a putt from the green hits the flagstick (whether it's in or out of the hole).

sure that everyone can clearly see the cup, take the flagstick out of the cup and set it off to the side. If the hole is hard to see, ask another player to "tend the flag." Tending the flag involves holding the flag against the stick and standing several feet to the side of the hole (away from the putt line). Also, make sure your shadow doesn't cover any part of the hole or the putt line. As the

ball rolls toward the hole, remove the flagstick. Once everyone has holed out, carefully return the flagstick to the hole and quickly move to the next hole. Mark your scores there. Do not linger on the green!

> ### ◆ QUICK TIP ◆
>
> It's not a penalty if your ball hits the flagstick ball when you're hitting from off the green. Play your ball where it lies.

"Mark your ball!"

When you reach the green, if your ball is in the way of another player's putt, quickly mark your ball and move it out of the way. Here's how: Set a coin or flat "marker" directly behind your ball and then lift your ball.

◀● If your mark happens to be right on your opponent's putt line, move it away using your putter head as a guide. To do this, place your putter head to the side of your current mark, align it with a landmark (a tree or bush), and then pick up your mark and move it to the other end of the putter head. After your opponent has finished putting, realign the putter head with the landmark, move the marker back to its original position, and replace your ball.

Hint: The USGA says that when marking your ball it's best to use a coin or flat ball marker, but you don't have to. You can also use a tee or the toe of your putter.

◈ QUICK TIP ◈

If there's a ball in your way, always ask the player to mark and move it. Why? It's a two-stroke penalty if a putt from the green hits another player's ball!

When you're walking on the green or taking your next stroke, don't step on the line of another player's putt! Many players feel this dents the turf, possibly causing the upcoming putt to jump off line and miss the cup. It's hard to know if it really does, but proper etiquette says to step across or walk around this area.

"Take care of the green!"

Almost every approach shot will leave a big "ball mark" on the green when it lands. When this happens (and it happens a lot), it's your responsibility to repair it. Here's how: Take a tee or forklike tool and poke it into the turf at an angle. Circle the ball mark, pushing the sunken turf back to the center. Then firmly tap it down with the bottom of your putter until it's level with the green. Remember, you'll get some extra luck if you fix your own ball mark and at least one other!

Lift the turf

Tap it level!

The good news? A ball mark that's repaired immediately heals in less than 24 hours. The bad news? A ball mark that's not fixed within an hour may take 15 days to heal!

In addition to being careful about fixing ball marks, you should also be careful not to drop your clubs or your bag on the green. If you use a pull-cart (which holds your bag), don't walk it across the green. If you use a motorized cart, always stay well to the side of the green. If you see spike marks caused by golf shoes, quickly tap them down with your putter after you hole out. Do everything you can to keep the greens as smooth and as nice as possible!

"Don't play slow!"

You need to play at a brisk pace so you don't hold up other golfers. Here's how: • Walk as fast as you can between each shot. • Decide which club you're going to use *before* you get to your ball. Select your club, take a practice swing or two, and hit your shot in 30 seconds or less! • Set your golf bag off to the side of the green that leads to the next hole. Clear the green as soon as possible! • Instead of writing down your score while standing on the green of the

next hole. • Look for a lost ball as quickly as possible. (The rules allow no more than 5 minutes.) • If there's an open hole in front of you (or you're looking for a lost ball), invite the group behind you to play through.

6. **"My friend was hit with a golf ball while he was out playing one day. Are there any safety tips I need to know about?"** The most important thing to do is to keep your head and follow these simple tips:

• Shout "Fore!" as loud as you can if your ball flies toward another player or group of players. If you hear someone yell "Fore!" in your direction, turn away and cover your head with your arms. • Always wait to play until the players in front are out of range. • Stay well to the side of other players in your group as they hit their shots. • To avoid serious eye injuries, don't hit broken tees, twigs, or small pebbles toward other players during practice swings. • If you use a motorized cart, strictly follow all cart rules and regulations. • Be careful when hitting near trees or other immovable objects. Your ball or a broken club can ricochet backward, easily harming you or other players. • If you get caught in a lightning storm, don't stand under tall objects (trees or power poles) or on high ground. Instead, take cover at a low point on the golf course, and stay down. Your best bet is to get off the course *before* the lightning storm arrives.

7. **"Can you give me just the basic rules of the game?"** Yes, here's a brief list to get you started. Many more rules are explained on Hole 17 of this guidebook and in the official USGA Rulebook (www.usga.org).

- After each shot, play your ball as it lies. Don't move, press down, or break anything growing except to fairly take your stance.
- At the beginning of each hole, tee your ball anywhere between the tee markers (not in front of them), and no more than two club-lengths behind the *front* edge of the markers.
- Re-tee your ball if it accidentally falls from the tee or is bumped off by your club before your *first* swing. (No penalty.)

take your ball back to its original spot. (No penalty.)

- It's fine to remove your ball from the green to clean it as long as you mark its position first.
- When putting from the green, don't let your ball hit the flagstick or another player's ball. (Two penalty strokes.)

◆▷ QUICK TIP ◁◆

It's a good idea to buy an official rules book from the USGA or from your local PGA professional. Keep a copy in your bag in case you need to look something up!

---

8. **"How can I get the most out of my golf lessons?"** Consider the following:

Focus on the basics! What's the secret to good golf? There really are no secrets! It is just a matter of learning and mastering some basic skills and golf fundamentals that really haven't changed since the game was first invented. Things like gripping the club correctly, taking an athletic stance, aiming on target, staying in balance, making a full shoulder turn, moving each body part in a set sequence, swinging through the ball, finishing the swing, and so on.

Keep things simple and think of no more than one swing skill or swing thought at a time. Thinking of a long list of "do's" and "don'ts" will only mix you up. Ask your instructor to help you identify your biggest swinging error, and then work to solve this problem first. Fix any little mistakes later. Trying to be perfect all at once can be confusing and frustrating. Take each skill or swing tip one at a time. Then practice it over and over until it becomes second nature.

Do the "Let's Practice!" activities. These step-by-step activities are fun and can make your practice time more meaningful. The goal is simple: To help you improve in the fastest and most effective way possible.

Read and study this guidebook whenever you get a chance. Hang on to this guide. Everything you really need to know is here. And what's nice is that it's pocket-sized, so you can take it wherever you go—to your golf class, golf lesson, or to the course. After each lesson, jot down helpful tips that work for you. When you play, carry this guidebook in your golf bag and use it as a handy reference.

Have fun! Bobby Jones said, "Practice must be interesting, even absorbing, if it is to be of any use." This is great advice! Set goals. Make a game out of it. Play fun competitions. Learn something new. Most importantly, relax, keep smiling, and have a good time!

9. **Should I stretch before I swing?** Yes! Stretching is often skipped over, but it's very important since it can reduce stiffness and help you swing smoothly. Here's how to do it: • Stretch your muscles by moving each body part slowly until you feel mild discomfort, but not pain. • Hold the stretch for 10 to 30 seconds and then repeat several times. • Avoid fast, bouncing movements. Relax and breathe normally as you go. • Enjoy yourself and make stretching a regular part of your golfing routine!

Before going to play or practice, take a few minutes and do these simple stretching exercises:

Back stretch

Back twist

Back stretch

Cat stretch (down) | Cat stretch (up)

Hamstring stretch | Back twist

After arriving at the course or practice range, do these warm-up exercises to get yourself ready to practice or play:

Body twist (right)

Body twist (left)

Overhead reach

Slowly swing two clubs

Note to lefties: The tips in this guidebook are written for right-handed players, so you'll need to reverse the instruction to fit your swing.

Common Goof-ups!

When you golf . . .

- ⊘ Don't forget to learn the lingo, keep score, and play by the rules.
- ⊘ Be careful not to bother other players when they're lining up their shots or making their strokes.
- ⊘ Don't hit until the group in front of you is out of the way.
- ⊘ Don't play too slow!
- ⊘ Don't step on the line of another golfer's putt.

- ⊘ Don't forget to rake sand bunkers, replace divots, and repair ball marks.
- ⊘ Don't forget to stretch and warm up before you play!

Recap

- Get to know the golf lingo so you can "talk the talk" out on the course.
- There are six different shots in golf: the drive, the approach shot, the chip, the pitch, the sand shot, and the putt.
- Follow all of the "social graces" and rules so you can play the game right.
- Always stretch and warm up before you hit the links.
- Keep things positive and have fun.

What Now?

Let's go to Hole 2 and learn the grip!

GETTING READY
TO SWING

2

GET A GRIP!

Good golf starts with a good grip.

—BEN HOGAN

Hey, I've Got a Question!

1. **"Why is it so important to take a good grip?"** Your hands are the vital link between your body and the club. So vital, in fact, that the grip is called the "steering wheel" of the golf swing! Misaligning your hands can easily mess up your swing and send your shots off in the wrong direction. Some sports

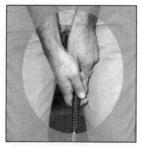

like baseball and racquetball don't require perfect grips, but in golf, taking a good grip is a key, fundamental skill!

2. **"There's more than one way to grip a club, isn't there?"** Yes. You can use the overlapping, interlocking, or ten-finger grip.

3. **"How do I choose a grip?"** It all depends on your unique pair of hands. Experiment a little to know which grip works best for you. Using the same grip as your friend or favorite player may not work because their hand size and structure may be much different than your own.

4. **"Is there a big difference between the three grips?"** No, not really. Other than the way you position the little finger of your right hand, the three grips are exactly the same. Take a minute and study the next three photos so you can understand the simple yet important differences between each grip.

◄● **Overlap grip:** Place the little finger of your right hand *over* the narrow groove between the first two fingers on your left hand. (Most PGA golf professionals and amateurs use this grip.)

♠ **Interlock grip:** Intertwine the little finger of your right hand *between* the first two fingers of your left hand and interlock them. (About 25 percent of golfers have a hand size that fits this type of grip.)

♠ **Ten-finger grip:** Set the little finger of your right hand directly on the club next to the first finger of your left hand so that all of your fingers contact the club. (A small number of golfers, usually young junior players, use this grip.)

⟫ QUICK TIP ⟪

Remember, you shouldn't choose a grip based on comfort alone. The key is to select a grip that fits your hand structure and lets you position your hands on the club correctly. For example, if the interlock grip feels good but doesn't let you grip correctly, you should use the overlapping grip instead.

5. "When I take my grip, what should my eyes be focusing on?" When lining up your club, always look at the leading or bottom edge of the clubface. Then it's easy to aim your clubface directly toward your target (so the clubface is squared or perpendicular to your aim line).

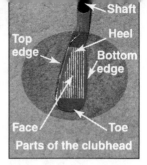

Parts of the clubhead

If you happen to look at the top edge of the clubface, you'll most likely aim the face to the left and hit shots that hook or curve from right to left.

6. "If my grip is correct, why doesn't it feel right?" Don't worry—a lot of golfers feel awkward, whether they're just learning the proper grip or trying to fix a grip that wasn't right. The reason the new grip feels so uncomfortable is because the muscles and nerves that control your hands and fingers are not yet trained to hold the club correctly. After about a week or so of practice, though, your muscles and nerves will "wake up," and your grip will begin to feel comfortable and strong. In fact, take some advice from Ben Hogan: "For at least a week put in 30 minutes of daily practice on the grip. Learning these next fundamentals [of the game] will then be twice as easy and twice as valuable."

> **• QUICK TIP •**
>
> The best way to train your hand muscles and nerves is to grip and regrip the club over and over again. Remember: The more practice repetitions you do, the faster you will learn the grip.

To Do It Right

When you take your grip . . .

Left Hand

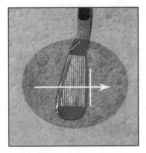

◀ **Square the clubface:** Set the bottom edge of your clubface square to your aim line.

Lock in left hand: With the back of your left hand facing the target, press the clubshaft under the muscle pad (just below the white "X") at the inside heel of your palm. ▶

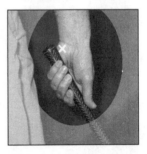

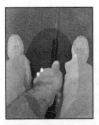

◀ **Look for two or two-and-a-half knuckles:** Position your hand so that when you look straight down you can see the first two or two-and-a-half knuckles on the back side of your left hand, but not the knuckle above the little finger; also extend your thumb down the shaft, just right of center.

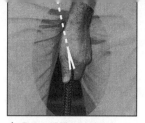

♠ **Point "V" to right shoulder:** Position your hand so the "V" formed by your thumb and first finger points to your right shoulder.

♠ **No gaps:** Be sure there are no spaces between the last three fingers of your left hand.

Right Hand

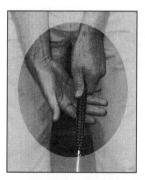

Hold club in fingers! With your right palm facing the target, situate the clubshaft more in the *fingers* of the right hand than in the palm; use either the overlap, interlock, or ten-finger grip based on the size of your hands.

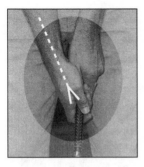

Cover your left thumb: Completely cover your left thumb with your right palm.

Point "V" to right shoulder: Extend your thumb down the shaft, just left of center so the "V" formed by the thumb and palm points to your right shoulder.

Hint: Does your "V" point to your right shoulder? If not, hold the club more in the fingers of your right hand or try a different grip (the overlapping, interlocking, or ten-finger grip), one that more closely matches your unique hand size.

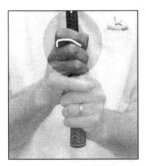

Form a trigger finger: For extra control, separate the index finger from the middle finger of your right hand so there is a small gap; this makes your index finger look like a "trigger-finger."

When you grip . . .

◎ Don't look at the top
edge of the clubface (this
causes you to aim your
clubface to the left of the
target); instead, always
look at the bottom edge!

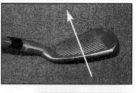

◎ Don't position the clubshaft above
the muscular pad of the left hand
(unless you're putting); instead
lock in your club under the X!

◎ Don't set your left hand so far to
the right that all four knuckles are
visible. Also called a "strong" grip.

◎ Don't point the "V" of the right
hand off to the side of the right
shoulder.

◎ Don't set your left hand so far to
the left that you can't see the first
two or two-and-a-half knuckles
on your left hand. Also called a
"weak" grip.

◎ Don't grip too tightly.

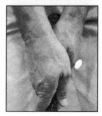

Recap

- Look at the bottom edge of the clubface as you align your club to the target.
- Use a grip that fits your hand size.
- Make sure the "V" of your right hand points to your right shoulder.
- Practice the correct grip every day until it feels comfortable and strong.

What Now?

Go to Hole 3 and learn the stance!

YOU'RE UP—TAKE THE RIGHT STANCE

If you set up correctly, there's a good chance you'll hit a reasonable shot, even if you make a mediocre swing. If you set up incorrectly, you'll hit a lousy shot even if you make the greatest swing in the world.

—JACK NICKLAUS

Hey, I've Got a Question!

1. **"How can I look like a pro when I'm getting ready to hit?"** Think for a minute about a quarterback ready to take a snap from center, or a tennis player ready to return a serve. Each has an athletic body posture—one that is relaxed but ready for action. The same is true with professional golfers.

To get into this athletic or power position, first set your feet about shoulder-width apart, with your weight evenly shared between each foot. Your weight should be over the middle of each foot—neither on your toes nor on the heels—so as to make you free to lift your heels or wiggle your toes, if desired.

Now, stick your buttocks out to the rear, like you are sitting on the edge of a waist-high bar stool. This is crucial and lets everything else fall into place. Now you can easily tilt your back forward a few inches, with the back mostly straight and not hunched over.

Lastly, bend your knees just enough to keep your legs relaxed and responsive. Also, let your arms and hands hang down just in front of your toes. Now you're ready for action, just like a PGA professional.

2. **"What should my feet be doing?"** The way you line up your feet determines your stance. In golf, there is an open stance, a closed stance, and a square stance.

Open stance

Closed stance

♠ For an open stance, the left foot is drawn several inches away from your aim line compared to your right foot. An open stance is commonly used on shorter shots that demand less power but excellent accuracy.

♠ For a closed stance, position your left foot a little closer to the aim line than the right foot so your stance line points a little to the right of the target. Very few golfers use this stance today.

Square stance

◖ The most common stance is a square one, with both feet the same distance from your aim line. This stance allows your lower body to contribute as much as your upper body to the swing, making it more powerful. Because of this, a square stance is recommended for all medium- and long-range shots.

Note: Instructions on how to aim are coming up in Hole 4.

Take the time to make sure your stance and posture are right, because even the slightest mistakes can cause major problems in your swing.

3. **"How far from the ball am I supposed to stand?"** Stand just far enough away so your arms hang almost straight down from your shoulders, with your hands just in front of your toes. This should put the end of your club about four to five inches (the width of your palm) from your left leg when using the shorter clubs and putter, and about six to eight inches (the width of two of your palms) when using the longer ones. Remember: Many players stand too far from the ball, which makes them overreach or hunch over too much.

4. **"When I'm taking swings on the range, should I hit my shots from off the turf or tee them up?"** Anytime you're working on your swing, it's important to keep things simple to build your confidence. For this reason, you might want to tee your ball (or at least make sure it's on a nice patch of grass) for all of your practice shots. Once you feel comfortable, you can make your practice shots more gamelike—with both good and bad lies. This type of "game-specific" practice is important because it teaches you how to handle any type of lie you might encounter out on the course.

5. **"Shouldn't my posture look a little different when I putt?"** Yes, it's not quite the same. When putting, it's okay to bend over from the belly so your eyes are directly over

your ball (so you can line up your shot). On all of the other shots, you need to stick your buttocks out, bend from the hips, and stand tall.

To Do It Right

When you take your stance . . .

Putting

Play the ball just inside your left foot, about one to two inches forward of center.

To promote good balance, set your feet about 12 inches apart.

Use a square stance.

Chipping

Play the ball back in your stance, across from your right ankle.

Set your heels a comfortable distance apart.

Place your right foot a little closer to the aim line than your left foot to open the stance slightly.

Short-Iron Shots (pitching wedge, 9-, or 8-iron)

Put the ball right in the middle of your stance (below your shirt buttons).

Put your feet about hip-width apart.

Use a slightly open stance.

Mid-Iron Shots (7-, 6-, or 5-iron)

Play the ball toward the front of your stance (in line with your shirt logo).

Set your feet a little wider than hip-width apart.

Use a square stance, with both feet the same distance away from the aim line.

Long Iron and Wood Shots (4-, 3-, 2-iron; fairway woods, driver)

Put your ball forward, across from your left heel.

Set your feet shoulder-width apart.

Use a square stance.

Other Options

There is a little wiggle room on where to play the ball across from your stance. If you want to hit your drive a little more on the upswing, play the ball forward in your stance (off your left toe). If you want to hit slightly down into the ball with your fairway woods, play the ball an inch back in your stance. Use the stance that works the best for you.

> **❖ QUICK TIP ❖**
>
> The direction you point your toes is also important. Most players turn the *left* or *front foot* out slightly. With the *right* or *back foot* you have the option to point it straight ahead or turn it out slightly.

To get the right amount of weight on each foot:

Put the same amount of weight on each foot.

Center the weight below your shoelaces—neither on your toes nor on your heels.

Other Options

Some instructors say to vary this a little—with a 60/40 split for your short irons and putter (or about 60 percent of your weight on your left foot and 40 percent on your right), a 50/50 split for your mid-irons, and a 40/60 split when using your long-irons and woods.

Common Goof-ups!

When getting ready . . .

⊘ Don't stand too tall, with your back not tilting forward enough.

⊘ Don't bend your knees too much or fail to stick out your buttocks enough. ➧

⊘ Don't play the ball too far back or too far forward in your stance.

ball; don't reach too far to get
your club to the ball. ◗

○ Don't put too much weight
on your toes instead of below
your shoelaces.

Recap

● In the stance for hitting with
a driver, set your feet about
shoulder-width apart, for a
wedge about hip-width apart.

● When using your long irons and woods, play the ball
up in your stance (across from your left heel); when
using your wedge and 9-iron, play the ball in the middle of your stance (below your shirt buttons).

● To get your posture right, stick your buttocks out first.
Then tilt your spine forward and bend your knees
slightly.

● Hang your hands down from your shoulders just in
front of your toes.

What Now?

Go to Hole 4 and learn
how to aim!

Go to Hole 4 and learn
how to aim!

> **JUST FOR FUN**
>
> "If you hit it to the right, it's
> called a slice. If you hit it to the
> left, it's called a hook. If you hit it
> straight, it's called a miracle." ●

4

READY, AIM . . .

I advocate aligning your feet, knees, and hips parallel to the target line.

—DAVID LEADBETTER

Hey, I've Got a Question!

1. **"Why is it so hard for me to tell where I'm aiming?"** Golfers have no other choice but to stand off to the side as we aim and swing. Other sports, like basketball, archery, or billiards, allow you to look straight down your aim line while you prepare to shoot. Can you imagine trying to

down the barrel? Well, that's what golfers have to do on every shot!

2. **"Do I aim up my stance straight for the target?"** Not really. Actually your stance line should point slightly to the left of your target and *not* directly at it. This is called aiming "parallel left," since your stance line is to the left but parallel to your aim line. A good way to visualize this concept is to think of a set of railroad tracks, with the inner track representing your stance line and the outer track representing your target line.

> ◆ **QUICK TIP** ◆
>
> One way to stop hitting shots to the right is to not point your stance line directly at your target. Instead, set your stance line "parallel left" of your target line.

3. **"How should I waggle my club before I swing?"** The waggle is an individual thing—there is really no one correct

> ⚓ **WORDS TO KNOW**
>
> **Aim line:** An imaginary line extending from your ball all the way to your target (sometimes called a "target line").
>
> **Stance line:** An imaginary line, extended across the toes, knees, hips, or shoulders, that's exactly parallel to the aim line.

way to do it. Some players like to gently hinge and un-hinge the wrists so the club-head moves slowly back and forth along the aim line a few inches, just behind the ball, while other golfers simply lift the clubhead up and down in a set rhythm. In the end, it doesn't matter what you do as long as it helps you relax and gets you ready for your up-coming shot.

All good players also jostle their feet up and down as they waggle the club. This is a good idea because it keeps the body moving and ready for the upcoming swing. To make this a habit, Ben Hogan says to practice the waggle and pre-swing routine for about 10 minutes a day, until it becomes automatic.

4. **"How many practice swings should I take before each shot? Any advice?"** Try not to take more than one or two practice swings; otherwise you may take too much time and slow down play. Interestingly, some professional golfers don't even take a single practice swing, since they play so often and have such good muscle memory. However, the average golfer needs to take a practice swing or two to help get ready for the upcoming shot.

5. **"Some players play so slow! Is there a time limit?"** There aren't any set rules (unless you're in a tournament), but you shouldn't play so slowly that you hold up other

All good basketball players have the same pre-shot routine before each free throw. Good golfers do the same. Once you decide on a routine that works for you, it's important to stick with it. Do the same thing before every shot. It will improve your ability to concentrate, make good decisions, and play with more consistency.

golfers. As talked about on Hole 1, walk as fast as you can, hit each shot in 30 seconds or less, clear the green as soon as possible, write down your score as you walk to the next hole, look as quickly as possible for lost balls, and invite faster groups to play through.

To Do It Right

When you aim . . .

First, aim your clubface to your target (square it with your aim line) before taking your grip!

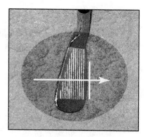

Is your clubface squared? After taking your grip, lift up your club so it's across from your chest. If the bottom edge of the clubface points straight up to the sky, it's squared and ready to go.

Second, set your feet, knee, and hip lines parallel to the aim line (the term for this is "parallel-left"—your body is lined up to the left of your aim line).

◆ QUICK TIP ◆

On longer shots, pick out an intermediate spot three to four feet in front of the ball, along your aim line. This gives a close-up guide that makes it easier to align your body parallel-left of the aim line.

Common Goof-ups!

When you aim . . .

- ⊘ Don't aim your stance line directly at your target; otherwise you'll actually be aiming off to the right. ➤

- ⊘ Don't do a different routine before each shot.

- ⊘ Don't take more than two practice swings or longer than 30 seconds before your shot.

- Aim parallel-left. Point your stance line parallel and to the left of your aim line.

- On longer shots, use an intermediate target (a spot a few feet in front of your ball) to help you aim.

- Play fast! Take only a couple of practice swings before each shot unless there's no one waiting.

JUST FOR FUN

"A young man with a few hours to spare one afternoon figures that if he hurries and plays very fast, he can get in 9 holes before he has to head home. As he is about to tee off, an old gentleman shuffles onto the tee and asks if he can join him. Although worried this will slow him up, the younger man says, "Of course." To his surprise, the old man plays quickly. He doesn't hit the ball very far, but it goes straight. Furthermore, the old man moves along without wasting any time. When they reach the ninth fairway, the young man is facing a tough shot. A large pine tree sits in front of his ball, directly between it and the green. After several minutes pondering how to hit the shot, the old man says, "You know, when I was your age, I'd hit the ball right over that tree." With the challenge before him, the young man swings hard, hits the ball, watches it fly into the branches, rattle around, and land with a thud a foot from where it had started. "Of course," says the old man, "when I was your age, that tree was only three feet tall." 🌟

What Now?

Go to Hole 5 and practice what you've learned.

5

LET'S PRACTICE!

Lessons are not to take the place of practice, but to make practice worthwhile.

—HARVEY PENICK

Grip

1. **Find the Right Tension.** Use one of your irons and practice gripping the club with various grip tensions. To do this, first use the lightest grip tension you can (about 20 percent of maximum tension), waggle the clubhead back and forth several times, and then remove your hands. Repeat this at 40, 60, 80, and 100 percent of your maximum tension—adding slightly more grip pressure as you go. Notice when it becomes difficult to waggle the club back and forth smoothly and freely. Most players like to keep their grip pressure somewhere between 70 and 80 percent of maximum.

Keep Sam Snead's famous example in mind: Grip the club as if you are holding a baby bird—apply just enough grip tension to hold the bird, but not so much that you do any harm to it.

2. **Practice Reps.** To practice the grip, carefully place your hands on the club's grip, waggle the clubhead back and forth a few times, and then remove your hands. Follow Ben Hogan's advice and practice this drill 10 minutes a day for at least a week. (You'll be glad you did.)

Stance and Posture

1. **Take the Right Stance.** Ask a partner to hand you any iron or wood, and then carefully practice the stance and posture for that specific club. Now, reach for another club and repeat the exercise. Keep going until you have practiced with a short-iron, mid-iron, long-iron, fairway wood, and your driver. Take turns as you go, and jot down helpful hints you want to remember.

Hint: For at least a week, practice the correct stance and posture for all of your clubs. Soon you'll do it without even thinking!

2. **Target Practice.** Aim at five different targets as your partner stands behind you (looking down your aim line). When you're ready, ask your partner to tell you where he or she thinks you are aiming, based on your clubface and body positions. See if your partner identifies the target you are aiming for. Jot down helpful hints you want to remember.

3. **Alignment Check.** Set two clubs on the ground parallel to one another, one club along your stance line and the other about 12 inches on the other side of your ball. Place each practice ball between the two clubs, identify an intermediate target several feet in front of your ball (along your aim line), and then carefully align your body parallel-left. Hit at least 10 shots with a short iron and at least 10 shots with a longer club.

Hint: You can also hold the shaft of a club across your knees, then hips, and then shoulders to make sure your entire body is aiming parallel-left.

The Goal: Take dead aim by aligning your body parallel-left.

▶ Quick Check

Show your instructor or partner your grip, stance, or aim and ask for feedback. Jot down helpful hints you want to remember:

THE SHORT GAME

CHIPPING—THE "BUMP-AND-RUN"

The shorter the shot, the more deliberate and carefully thought out your efforts must be.
—HENRY LONGHURST

Hey, I've Got a Question!

1. **"What does a chip shot look like?"** As mentioned in Hole 1, it's a low, bump-and-run shot that flies a short distance (just enough to get over grass that is too long to putt across), and then rolls most of the way to the hole.

2. **"How should I swing when I'm chipping?"** Use a short swing and keep your wrists steady during the entire swing. Just let the rocking motion of your shoulders move your arms back and forth. What about the knees? On the way back keep them steady; on the way through let them move

gently toward the target. Hit
the ball cleanly, with a downward blow.

3. **"Should I always chip
with the same club, or does it
matter?"** Most pros use any
one of several different clubs
(5-, 6-, 7-, 8-, 9-iron, or
pitching wedge), depending
on the ball's lie, slope of the
terrain, and distance from the
hole. Don't sweat it, though!

After plenty of practice you'll learn which club is right for
each situation.

4. **"How do I hit my chips the right distance?"** There are
two ways. First, adjust the length of your swing to match
the distance of the shot—a shorter swing for a 10-yard shot
and a longer swing for a 20-yard shot. Second, play a more
lofted club (pitching wedge or 9-iron) for shorter chips; a
less lofted one (7- or 8-iron) for longer chips.

◆ QUICK TIP ◆

Think of the face of a clock to help you gauge the length of your
swing. Here's an example: On short chips, swing back to about
7 or 8 o'clock (with your hands starting at 6 o'clock), and then
change directions and swing down and through to about 5 or
4 o'clock. To hit longer shots: Move a little farther back and forth
around the clock.

---

5. **When is the bump-and-run the best shot to hit?** It's a great shot when: • your ball is close to the green (within 5 to 10 feet) and sitting on short grass • your ball can easily reach the green, without getting caught up in any long grass or rolling into a hazard • the green is firm, so your ball can roll most of the way to the hole • hitting from a down slope or to a green with an uphill slope • the wind is gusting and you want to keep your ball down low.

To Do It Right

When you take your stance . . .

Stand tall; bend at the hips (stick your bum out); keep your back straight.

Hang your arms straight down from your shoulders (with your hands just in front of your toes). Slant your hands to the left, well ahead of the ball.

Grip down close to the metal of the shaft for better control and accuracy. Keep the club-face facing the target (as you slant your hands to the left).

Take an open stance with the ball across from your right ankle (this encourages a downward swing into the ball). Put a little more weight on your front foot.

When you chip . . .

On the Way Back

Rock shoulders back

Keep wrists steady (no hinging!) ➡

Swing hands between 7 and 8 o'clock (6 o'clock being straight down)

Knees stay steady (don't shift weight!)

On the Way Through

Rock shoulders through

Keep arms relaxed (fingers stay secure)

Swing down and through (stop at about 5 or 4 o'clock)

Knees move softly

Hold follow-through (hands stay ahead of clubhead) ➡

When you chip, try to swing your arms back and forth about the same distance. But don't worry if the grass grabs your club and shortens the length of your follow-through a little.

Common Goof-ups!

When you chip . . .

🚫 Don't play the ball too far forward in your stance. ➡

🚫 Don't swing too fast on the way back.

🚫 Don't take a backswing that's too long for the needed distance. ➡

🚫 Don't flip your wrists on the way through.

Recap

- Hit a chip when your ball is close to the green, on short grass, and there's not a hazard between you and the hole.

- Play the ball back in your stance. Slant your hands to the left, well ahead of the ball.

- Keep your wrists steady on the way back and on the way through. Let your shoulders control the swing.

- Hit the ball cleanly, with a downward blow.

- To chip it longer, take a slightly longer swing or hit a less lofted club.

What Now?

Go to Hole 7 and learn how to pitch!

7

PITCHING—THE "LOB"

The common error is taking the club back too far and decelerating through impact, which is like a boxer pulling his punches. It causes all sorts of mishit and misdirected pitch shots.

—Tom Watson

Hey, I've Got a Question!

1. **"Can you explain a pitch shot to me?"** As mentioned on Hole 1, a pitch is a high-flying, quick-stopping shot that flies most of the way to the hole and rolls only a short distance. Pitch shots range from fairly short (just off the green) to the length of a football field (about 100 yards away from the flag).

2. **"How should I swing when I hit a pitch shot?"** To get the height you need, use a lofted club (pitching, lob, or sand wedge), and move your wrists smoothly during the swing.

Relax and feel it! To dial in the right distance, adjust the length of your swing to match the distance of the shot.

3. **"When is the pitch shot the best shot to use?"** It's a great shot when: • your ball is in longer grass and you need to cut through the grass to get to your ball • your ball needs to fly up and over a sand bunker or hazard that is situated between you and the hole • the green is soft, not allowing much roll.

4. **"Is there a secret to hitting high, fast-stopping pitch shots?"** These shots, sometimes called "flop" shots, fly higher, roll less, and stop sooner if your ball has more backspin. What you need to know is how to increase the backspin. Here's the secret: Before taking your grip, turn open the clubface of your sand or lob wedge so it faces the sky. Take a long, lazy swing. Hinge and unhinge the wrists freely. Swing the clubface steeply down into the ball (to pinch the ball between your clubface and the grass). You might also try using a faster-spinning ball with a softer cover.

Hint: To do this shot you need a good lie, with your ball sitting up in medium-length grass. It's best if there's little or no grass right behind your ball—this gives your clubface room to slide cleanly under the ball. If your ball's on really short grass (sometimes called a "thin lie"), the bottom of your clubface might hit the middle of the ball and send it flying over the green! If your ball's in the long stuff, ball. This makes it hard to create backspin and hit your ball the right distance.

To Do It Right

When you take your stance . . .

Stand tall, bend at the hips (stick your buttocks out), and keep your back straight.

Hang your arms straight down from your shoulders, just in front of your toes. Set your hands even with or slightly behind the ball.

Grip down a few inches for better control and accuracy. Turn open the clubface the right amount, depending on how far you want the shot to go.

Take an open stance with the ball in the middle of your stance. Place an even amount of weight on each foot.

When you pitch . . .

On the Way Back

Rock shoulders back

Hinge wrists smoothly
(swing your hands between
8 and 10 o'clock, form an
"L" between your left arm
and club) ●▶

Knees stay soft

On the Way Through

Keep arms relaxed (fingers
stay secure)

Swing freely

Keep knees responsive

Hold follow-through (stop
at about 2 o'clock or so) ●▶

●▶ **QUICK TIP** ◀●

Like in chipping, adjust the length of your swing to match the
distance of the shot—a shorter swing for a 25-yard pitch and a
longer swing for a 50-yard pitch.

Common Goof-ups!

When you pitch . . .

- 🚫 Don't play the ball too far forward in your stance.

- 🚫 Don't take a backswing that is too long for the needed distance and then quit or stop too soon on the way through.

- 🚫 Don't swing too fast on the way back.
- 🚫 Don't hit too far behind the ball or hit the top of the ball.

Recap

- Hit a pitch when your ball is close to the green, on long grass, or there's a hazard between you and the hole.

- Play the ball in the middle of your stance. Use a slightly open stance.

- Let your wrists hinge and unhinge freely during the swing.

- Accelerate and swing smoothly on the way through.

What Now?

Go to Hole 8 and learn how to putt!

JUST FOR FUN

After slicing his tee shot into the woods, a golfer heads off in search of his ball, which he finds behind a large tree. After considering his position—and not wanting to take a drop and lose a stroke—he decides to hook the ball around the tree. He swings, the ball hits the tree, ricochets back at him, and instantly kills him. When he opens his eyes, he sees the Pearly Gates and St. Peter standing before him. "Am I dead?" he asks. "Yes, my son," replies St. Peter, who looks the man over and notices his clubs. "I see you're a golfer," St. Peter says. "Are you any good?" "Hey, I got here in two, didn't I?"

8

PUTTING—THE SECRET TO LOW SCORES

The key to good putting is comfort and confidence.
—BILLY CASPER

Hey, I've Got a Question!

1.   "Why is good putting the secret to low scores?" There's an old saying that goes like this: "Drive for show and putt for dough." No doubt, it is impressive to hit a nice 300-yard drive, but the best way to "take home the dough" is to make your putts. Holing a long putt instantly shaves strokes off your score! In golf, a short three-foot putt counts the same as a long drive—one stroke. So, if you make the long putts and don't have to take the short ones, there's not a better way to lower your score!

2. "I've noticed a lot of different putting grips. Which one do you think I should use?" Any kind of putting grip is fine as long as it's comfortable, but most good players like to use the "reverse-overlapping" grip. To hold your putter this way, first put on a normal overlapping grip and then switch the position of your right little finger and left index finger. This puts all the fingers of your right hand on the club, while the index finger of your left hand rests over the little or ring finger of your right hand.

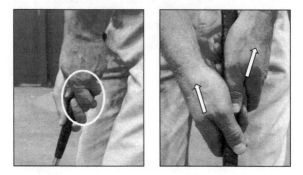

One more thing: Grip the putter so your palms face one another and the "V" of the left hand points to the left shoulder and the "V" of the right hand points to the right shoulder.

3. "How should I swing when I putt?" A smooth pendulum stroke works best. To putt this way, let your shoulders and arms rock back and forth to move the pendulum—just like a grandfather clock swinging back and forth. The wrists stay steady (with no hinging), and the hips and legs

should stay quiet and motionless, too. Although it may seem a little awkward at first (with your shoulders, arms, and hands all moving together at the same time), it's the best way to putt.

4. **"How do I learn to hit putts the right distance?"** Adjust the length of your stroke to match the distance of your putt. Use a shorter stroke for a 3-foot putt and progressively longer ones for 6-, 9-, 12-, and 15-foot putts. Also, try to make the amount of time for each stroke the same, even though the length of the stroke changes.

❖ QUICK TIP ❖

To get your ball to roll as far as it should, make the swing through at least as long as or longer than the swing back. Hit the ball near the center or "sweet spot" of your putterface. (The sweet spot on your putter is usually marked with a white line or dot on the top of the putterhead.)

---

5. **"How can I get my putts to go right where I want them to?"** If the green is flat and smooth, your ball will find the target if you do two things: First, keep your putter squared to the aim line as you hit the ball. Second, swing the putter directly toward the target as you swing through.

How's it done? Use a pure pendulum stroke with absolutely no forearm turning or wrist hinging during the whole stroke. This perfect stroke takes the putter straight back and through, with the ball rolling right into the hole.

• QUICK TIP •

Dave Pelz recently discovered this interesting fact: The angle of the putterface as it hits the ball (whether it be open, closed, or squared) is four times more important in sending the ball in a given direction than the path of the putter as it swings into the ball. The bottom line: If you want to sink your putts, keep the putter squared to the aim line!

---

6. **"Besides using a pendulum putting stroke and keeping my grip pressure just right, are there any other secrets I should know?"** Yes, here are a few more to consider:

Spot putt: When lining up your putt, find a spot along your putt line that is somewhere between your ball and the hole. Then aim at that spot in the same way that a bowler aims at a spot (or an intermediate target) on the lane between the foul line and the pins. The spot can be a discoloration on the green or an imaginary spot, and can be located anywhere along your putt line—from several inches to several feet from your ball. On longer putts, two or more spots can help you see your entire aim line.

deciding where to aim, take a moment and look from behind your ball (down your aim line) to see any slopes or undulations in the green. If you are still unsure where to aim, walk past the hole and then back to your ball so you can view your putt from different angles.

Hit every putt straight: Even if your ball will curve (or "break") as it rolls to the target, always aim for a selected spot or target that is straight ahead (or so many inches above or below the hole). It's always easier to aim along a straight line than down a curving one.

Watch every chip and putt: Always notice the roll direction of all prior chips or putts as they approach or roll past the hole, since this gives you helpful clues on how to aim your next shot.

Softly hit putts break more; firmly hit putts break less: Because gravity has more time to work on the ball, a softly stroked putt curves or breaks more than a firmly stroked putt. For this same reason, longer putts break more than shorter putts.

Don't forget: On the same amount of slope, a putt on a fast, dry green breaks more than on a putt on a slow, wet green; a downhill putt breaks more than an uphill putt; a putt going with the grain of the green (the same direction the grass lays down) breaks more than a putt going against the grain.

When you putt out on the course, think mostly about your aim line and where you want your ball to end up, rather than the mechanics of your stroke. On short putts, focus on the direction of the putt and the exact line you want your ball to roll on. On long putts, focus mostly on the distance and the speed of the putt, with the goal to hit your ball within a 2-foot circle of the hole.

New trends: Here are four new putting styles some pros and amateur players like to use. Give each one a test run and see what you think. (*Note:* The last two methods require you to use a longer than normal putter.)

◆ "Left Hand Low" Grip
Place your left hand below your right. Overlap your left pinky between the first two fingers of your right hand. Take a normal stroke.

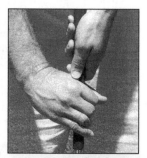

"Claw" Grip Regrip your right hand so it looks like a claw. Swing the putter back and forth with your left hand; let your right hand go along for the ride. ◆

◄• **Body Putter** Bend over as usual. Anchor the butt of the putter to your belly or chest; use the grip of your choice; take a normal stroke.

Long Putter Stand tall. Anchor the butt of the putter to your chest or chin with your left hand; swing the putter back and forth with your right hand. •➡

Note: Dave Pelz has done lots of research on the traditional way most golfers putt, as well as these four new putting styles. His results, based on thousands of golfers, show how each method stacks up on both straight and breaking putts. What's intriguing is that the body putter method comes out on top as the best way to make 3- and 9-foot putts and the second-best way to make 18-footers and lag 30-footers, while the traditional method was the worst of the bunch in holing the shorter putts (3- and 9-feet), but the best way to hole 18-footers and lag 30-footers. So based on these results, it looks like the traditional method carries the day on the longer putts, but doesn't shine as bright on the shorter ones. Of course, who's to say which method is best for you? The only way to find out is to give each method a try and see which one you like the most.

To Do It Right

When you take your stance...

◄• Use a square stance. Play the ball just inside your left foot about 1 or 2 inches forward of center (and about 10 inches out in front of your stance line).

Put the same amount of weight on each foot.

tice how your arms and shoulders form a triangle).

Take a comfortable grip.

Position your hands even with or just ahead of the ball, with the wrists arched slightly upward (away from the body). ➤

Set the putter behind (almost touching) your ball. Make sure the putterface is squared to your aim line.

◀ Bend from the waist just enough so your eyes are above (or an inch to the inside of) the aim line. *Hint:* How much you bend over depends on the length of your arms, legs, and torso.

Ideally, set your hands so they hang below your shoulders.

When you putt...

On the Way Back

Rock shoulders back

Maintain the triangle

◆ Keep wrists steady (no hinging!)

Keep arms relaxed (fingers stay secure)

Swing straight back

Knees stay steady

Watch your wrists a few times while you putt and make sure they stay steady the entire stroke. If you hinge your wrists, it's easy to open or close the putterface, which sends your putt off in the wrong direction.

On the Way Through

Rock shoulders through

Maintain the triangle

◀◉ Keep wrists steady (no hinging!)

Keep arms relaxed (fingers stay secure)

Swing straight through

Hold follow-through

When putting, take it back and through about the same length. Don't stop your follow-through too soon! Plus, always feel the rhythm of the swing.

Common Goof-ups!

When you putt . . .

- ⊘ Don't stand too far from the ball. Instead set your eyes above the ball.

- ⊘ Don't stand too close to the ball.
- ⊘ Don't set your hands too close to your body.

- Don't flip your wrists on the way through. Instead, keep them steady the whole time! ➧

- Don't move your knees on the way back or on the way through.

- Don't swing back too far for the needed distance and then stop too soon on the way through.

- Don't aim to the right or left and then swing the putter across the ball to bring it back to the hole. ➧

- Don't change your grip pressure during any part of the stroke.

- When you putt out on the course, think only about your aim line and where you want your ball to end up. Don't think about your stroke or you'll become too mechanical and stiff.

Recap

- Set your eyes above (or just inside) your aim line.

- Let your shoulders control the stroke. Keep your body steady.

- Swing the putter straight back and straight through.

- Take a short stroke on short putts, a long stroke on long putts.

- Always feel the rhythm of the swing.

- When you play, think mostly about your aim line and where you want your ball to end up.

- Play every putt as if it were straight. Pick the highest point along your aim line and try to roll your ball over that spot.

- Hit each putt the right speed so your ball curves the right amount and rolls the right distance. Remember the old saying: "Never up, never in!"

> **JUST FOR FUN**
>
> What are the four worst words you could hear during a game of golf? It's still your turn!

What Now?

Go to Hole 9 and practice what you've learned.

9

LET'S PRACTICE!

The more I practice, the luckier I get.
—GARY PLAYER

Chipping

1. **Target Practice.** Chip practice balls with your 7-, 8-, or 9-iron. Keep going until you can hit five in a row within a 6-foot circle.

2. **Cluster Drill.** Find a place just off the practice green where the grass is fairly short. Use your 7-, 8-, or 9-iron. Get a small bucket of balls and hit short, medium, and long chip shots. Try to cluster the balls into three separate groups (about 15 feet apart).

Intermediate Drill: Once your distance control improves, try the ladder drill. To do this, hit five chip shots, making each shot go about two to three feet farther than the prior shot simply by changing the length of your stroke. You'll know you are getting good when each ball stops only a few feet apart.

The Goal: Hit your chips the right distance.

> ◆ QUICK TIP ◆
>
> Try to keep your chip shots as low as possible, because the lower the ball flies, the easier you can control the distance.

Pitching

1. **Cluster Drill.** Use a pitching wedge, sand wedge, or 9-iron. Get a small bucket of balls and hit short, medium, and long pitch shots. Try to cluster the balls into three separate groups (about 10 to 15 yards apart) simply by changing the length of your swing. You can also take the same length of a swing, but turn the clubface open different amounts (before you take your grip) to practice hitting your ball a different height and distance.

> ◆ QUICK TIP ◆
>
> How does a chip differ from a pitch? When chipping, play the ball well back in your stance and keep your wrists steady. When pitching, play the ball in the middle of your stance and let your wrists cock smoothly.

(pitching wedge or 9-iron), to a target about 30 yards away. Try to hit each shot as close to the target as possible. Keep going until you can hit five in a row within a 10-yard circle.

> **Did You Know?** Your best chance of making a putt is if it's inside ten feet of the hole. And how do you get there? The wedges, pitches, chops, and bunker shots of your short game.
>
> —Dave Pelz

Putting

1. **Partner Check.** Stand about five feet from a hole and have a partner crouch down behind your ball (along your aim line) and check your aim, using the following two tips:

- The putterface is squared and pointing at the target.
- Your feet, knees, and hips are lined up parallel to and left of the aim line.

Now, go ahead and hit your putt. Ask your partner to check your aim and whether or not your putter moved straight back and straight through as you hit the ball. Use this feedback to improve your putting skills.

Hint: Ask your partner to hold a clubshaft just above your ball (down the target line) so you can see exactly where you're aiming.

2. **Putt Down the Alley.** Make an alleyway with two irons pointing toward the cup. Set the irons just far enough apart so your putter fits in between. Practice hitting putts without the putter touching either shaft. A second option is to set two tees in the green slightly wider than your putter. Practice hitting short and long putts, without touching either tee.

3. **Putt Over a Spot.** Set a ball mark or coin on the green a few feet ahead of your ball, just to the side of your aim line. See how many putts you can roll just to the side of your ball mark along the way to your ultimate target.

The Goal: Aim up your putts by using an intermediate target (a discoloration or spot) on the green.

◆ QUICK TIP ◆

As you line up a putt, it's crucial to see an imaginary line or alleyway from your ball to the hole. This tells your body exactly what it should do to stroke your ball into the hole.

4. **Circle the Hole.** Pair up with a partner and see who can make the most putts from at least five different positions around the cup. Circle the hole as many times as you can in 10 minutes. ➠

➠ **QUICK TIP** ➠

To correctly read each putt's break, imagine the direction a stream of water would flow into the cup from that exact spot. Try to hit your putt on that same path.

5. **Cluster Drill.** Get a small bucket of balls. Hit short, medium, and long putts and try to cluster the balls into three groups (about 10 feet apart).

➠ **Intermediate Drill:** Set five practice balls on the green about two feet apart along a straight line. Begin on either end and stroke the first ball so it rolls just a few feet ahead to a given spot on the green; then move back to the next ball and try to hit this putt as close as possible to the first ball. Continue moving back, trying to hit each putt as close as possible to the first ball simply by increasing the length of your stroke to match the length of each putt.

Hint: Ask a partner to crouch down across from you and make sure the length of your stroke gets a little longer as you move farther from the target.

The Goal: Hit your putts the right distance.

6. **Lag It Close!** Place five practice balls about 30 feet (10 paces) away from your target. Pair up and have your partner stand near your target. Hit each putt, immediately close your eyes, and then without looking tell your partner where you think your putt ended up in relation to your target (short and right, long and left, and so forth).

The Goal: Sense where your putt will end up based on how the stroke feels when you hit the ball.

7. **Seven-Up.** Pair up with a partner and play seven-up on the practice putting green. After deciding on the target, one point is earned for each one-putt, zero points for each two-putt, and minus one point for each three-putt. Putt to a different hole after each point (and take turns selecting the next target). The first player to earn seven points (or be seven points ahead) wins the match. *Hint:* Go with short putts when you hope to earn points and longer ones when you're behind and want your partner to three-putt and lose points.

✔ Quick Check

Show your instructor or partner your chipping, pitching, and putting stroke and ask for feedback. Jot down helpful hints you want to remember.

THE FULL SWING

10

THE SWING'S THE THING

Naturally you have to learn the various parts of the golf swing. But once you get it, don't think about your swing anymore.

—Sam Snead

Hey, I've Got a Question!

1. "What should I think about while I'm swinging?" What you think about depends on your goals and current skill level. Here's a guide:

- **Need to fix part of your swing?** Keep things simple and think of just one swing thought during each swing. When you feel like you've got it, see if you can swing correctly without thinking about it. As time goes on, if you slip back into an old swing rut (don't worry, it's very common), simply go back to your helpful swing thought until you get back on track. As you continue to practice and improve, focus on those swing thoughts that help you the most.

- **Playing on the course?** On each shot, focus on your aim line and what you want to accomplish. Save your swing-fixing thoughts for the practice range. Exception: If you find a single swing thought that really works for you out on the course, keep using it.
- **All the time!** If you think of too many swing thoughts at once, you'll tie yourself up in knots. Don't lose the feel of your swing. Find a perfect balance between thinking about what you're doing and "feeling" the swinging motion. Once you get the swing down, go on automatic pilot and let it freewheel!

2. **"How fast should I swing?"** While the backswing is slow and smooth, the forwardswing is powerful and accelerating. To help you swing at the right pace, here are a few trusty tips:

- **Think "low and slow."** As you swing away, keep your wrists steady (for a foot or so) and slowly brush across the top of the grass with your clubhead.
- **Don't rush.** Gradually turn your shoulders and lift your arms upward. Stay relaxed. Think smooth and easy.

On the Way Through

- **Hear the swoosh.** For each practice swing, swing fast enough so you can hear a loud swoosh sound on the way through. If you don't hear it, swing your body and arms faster!
- **Swing through the ball, not at it**. Surprisingly, your club should be moving at its fastest speed several feet after it hits the ball.

- **Don't tense up too much.** Stay relaxed! Tensing up your shoulders, arms, or grip actually slows down the club and drastically hurts your power and accuracy.
- **Feel the weight of your club.** If you can sense the weight of the club as you swing, it shows that your arms are relaxed and responsive.

◆ QUICK TIP ◆

As you complete your backswing, don't feel rushed as your arms change direction! To get the right pace, say "O-N-E and two" to yourself as you swing back and through.

---

3. **"It's hard to keep my balance during the swing. Any advice?"** You bet! Balance during the swing is crucial. Just watch the pros and notice their perfect balance. Practice these three tips to help you do the same:

- Keep your head steady and stay at the same height during the entire swing. Avoid lifting or dipping your head!
- Don't lift your left heel off the ground on the way back.
- Don't sway your hips too much on the way back. Instead, turn your hips as your arms swing to the top.

4. **"My Dad told me to keep my left arm straight on the way back. Is this right?"** A wide, circular swing is very important, but if you keep your left arm too straight or rigid it may hurt your swing. Here's a happy medium that works for most players: Keep your left arm as straight as possible, but not locked at the elbow or tense at any time.

5. **"How high should I swing my hands on the way back?"** To help players understand this, Ben Hogan said to imagine a tall glass window extending up from the ball and leaning against the golfer's shoulders (with a hole to slip the

head through). A correct swing path is accomplished when your arms, at least during the second half of the backswing, swing as close as possible to the imaginary window without touching it. Done right, your hands should be swung directly across from the tip of your right shoulder by the time you reach the top of your backswing.

Swinging your arms too far below the window (a "flat" swing) looks like a baseball swing and often leads to topped shots or shots that fly too low. On the flipside, breaking through the imaginary window by swinging the arms too high above the glass is called an "upright" swing and often leads to fat or chunked shots or shots that pop up or slice.

◆ **QUICK TIP** ◆

To know if your swing path is correct, do what David Leadbetter suggests: "Swing to the top of a full swing and stop. Slowly loosen your grip, and let the shaft fall. If the club hits you on the tip of your right shoulder, your swing is on plane."

As you take it to the top, here are a few more tips to help you get on track: Swing the club away with your arms and shoulders (keep your wrists steady). Move the club slowly and keep it close to the ground for the first foot or so.

When your hands are between 8 and 9 o'clock, the toe of the club points to the sky. ➠

◀ When your hands are at 9 o'clock, the shaft points down to the ball or target line.

6. **"Does it matter how I cock my wrists on the way back?"**
Yes. After you swing the club away from the ball a foot or so,
begin to smoothly turn your forearms and cock your wrists.

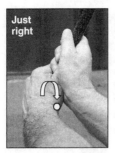

◄ As you cock your wrists, let your left hand move directly toward the base of your left thumb (to the dot). This slightly cups the backside of the wrist, forming the deepest wrinkles at the base of the left thumb. No wrinkles (or only slight ones) should form along the palm- or backside of the left wrist.

Cupping the left wrist too much on the way back flares the knuckles out even more; this usually opens the clubface and leads to slicing problems. ▶

◄ Bowing the wrist the other way turns the knuckles of the left hand under too much; this closes the club-face and leads to hooking problems.

The Bottom Line: If your left wrist cups too much on the way back you may need to adjust your grip. For example, put on your normal grip with the end of your club pointing to your belly button. If you can see three or more knuckles on your left hand, you may have it turned too far to the right. This makes your left wrist cup too much during the backswing. Is this a bad thing? Probably, since most pros don't do it. Of course, your best bet is to use the recommended grip. Then your left wrist can cock the right way (toward the *base* of your left thumb) and it'll be easier to hit straight shots. Once you've got this down (and the club's toe points to the sky as your arms go past 8 o'clock on the way back), the next part of the backswing is a snap: Simply continue turning your shoulders and lifting your arms as you swing to the top.

7. **"Should I keep my head down through the whole swing?"** Surprisingly, you shouldn't. After hitting the ball, your head should swivel so you can watch the flight of your ball. In fact, notice how the head moves forward directly above the front foot. ❧

To Do It Right

When you take your stance . . .

◄● Hang your arms almost straight down from your shoulders, with your hands just in front of your toes.

Stick your buttocks out, tilt your back forward as a unit, and bend your knees slightly.

Lift your chin up a little.

Notice how the right shoulder is slightly lower than the left. This happens because the right hand is lower on the grip than the left. ●►

Keep your left arm straight but re-laxed. Bend your right arm a little so it points to your right hip.

Angle your hands toward the target so they're slightly in front of your clubhead (in other words, when you look down at your clubhead, your hands are a little to the left).

When you swing . . .

On the Way Back

◄► Swing club away low and slow
(stay relaxed!)

Wrists stay steady (for a foot or so)

Hinge wrists smoothly (when your
hands reach about 9 o'clock, form an
"L" between your left arm and club) ◆►

Hands swing upward (as shoulders
turn)

◆► QUICK TIP ◆►

Some advanced players like to complete the wrist hinge (make
the "L") a bit later on the way back—somewhere between
10 o'clock and the top of the swing. So when you've got a good
swing, see if delaying your wrist hinge a little on the backswing
gives you the results you want.

Top of the Swing

◄● Turn back to target (the left shoulder turns under the chin)

Extend left arm

Load weight on right side ●►

Stay in perfect balance

On the Way Through

Arms stay relaxed (fingers are secure)

Hear the swoosh (feel the speed!)

Hold follow-through (belt buckle points left of the target)

Common Goof-ups!

When you swing . . .

- ⊘ Don't hinge your wrists too soon on the way back. Swing your hands, arms, and shoulders as a unit and keep your wrists steady for the first foot or so.

- ⊘ Don't swing away too far inside or outside. Instead swing straight back the first foot or so; then gradually move the club to the inside.

- ⊘ Don't bend your left elbow too much (like a baseball swing), with your hands drawing in too close to the right shoulder.

- ⊘ Avoid what's called a "chicken-wing" swing. Instead, keep your elbows and forearms the same distance apart during the whole swing!

- ⊘ Don't fan the clubface open too far on the way back. Instead point the toe of the club to the sky.

◆ QUICK TIP ◆

To stop fanning the clubface open so far, try this: As you swing away and hinge your left wrist, turn your knuckles under a little instead of letting them flare out.

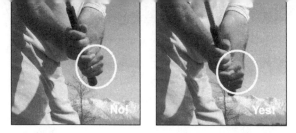

- ⊘ Don't swing too fast on the way back or too slow on the way through.
- ⊘ Don't loosen your left- or right-hand grip at the top of the swing. ➠

- ⊘ Don't lose your balance.
- ⊘ Don't swing the arms around too low (or up too high) on the way back. ➠

- ⊘ Don't keep your head and eyes down the entire swing. Instead, look up and watch the flight of the ball. ➡

- ⊘ Don't think of more than one swing thought at a time. Always feel the rhythm of the swing!

Recap

- Swing the club away from the ball low and slow.
- Keep your left arm as straight as you can (without tensing it up) on the way back.
- When you reach 8 and 9 o'clock, make sure the club's toe points to the sky.
- Keep your elbows the same distance apart during the whole swing.
- Stay in perfect balance.
- Swing through the ball, not at it!
- When you're trying to fix your swing, think of just one thing at a time.

What Now?

Go to Hole 11 and learn how to hit it long and straight!

11

HIT IT LONG
AND STRAIGHT

You must try to keep the golf swing as simple as you can.
That is why I'm so adamant about fundamentals.
—KATHY WHITWORTH

Hey, I've Got a Question!

1. **"I'm fighting a terrible slice! Any hope?"** Yes! There are
a lot of reasons why your shots go where they do (your grip,
aim, and swing balance to name a few), but let's talk about
the two most important for fixing your slice.

Rolling the Forearms—for Better Accuracy

In slow motion, it's easy to see how the clubface opens and closes during the swing. It's much like a door swinging open and shut. Just after you begin the swing, the forearms gradually roll (clockwise) and turn the clubface open on the way back. Then, on the way down, you reverse the process. If everything goes well (your wrists hinge right and your forearms roll exactly the same amount in both directions), the clubface will return to the ball in a squared position, and your shot will fly straight.

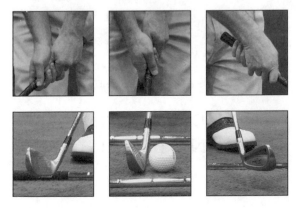

Even after hitting the ball, the forearms and clubface keep turning as you swing into your follow-through. This means that the ball is hit while the clubface turns (from an open-to-closed position) and hopefully spins into the ball at just the right moment. If the clubface turns a little too fast or a little too slow, your shot will hook off to the clubface when it hits the ball.

The only way to hit straight shots is to turn open the clubface just the right amount on the way back, and then spin the clubface freely back into the ball on the way through. You're not the only golfer having trouble doing one or both of these. Some players fan the clubface too far open on the way back, and then can't spin the clubface fast enough on the way down to make up for the mistake. Their clubface hits the ball in an open position and their shot slices off to the right.

Other golfers open the clubface the right amount on the way back, but then hold on too tight and don't spin (or close) the clubface quickly enough on the way down. The ball is hit with an open clubface, and their shot slices off to the right.

While many golfers fight a slice, just as you are, others fight a hook. Hooking problems happen when the clubface is not turned open enough on the way back or when the clubface turns too quickly into the ball on the way down (a rare problem).

How can you fix your slice and hit straight shots? Go to Hole 12 and practice the 9 o'clock, split-hands, heavy club, and toe-in drills.

Swinging with Good Timing—for Better Accuracy

The timing of your downswing also has a big influence on the accuracy of your shots. If your hips race too far ahead of the upper body and your arms lag behind, it's impossible to square up the clubface soon enough to hit a straight shot. When this happens, the arms are so far behind and can't roll into the ball fast enough, and your shot will usually slice off to the right (sometimes called a "blocked" swing).

On the flipside, if your shoulders and arms start the downswing (a.k.a. "shoulder dive") instead of your hips, the arms nearly always pull the club across the ball (an out-to-in path), and your shots veer off to the left. This is a common problem when the downswing is rushed and the hips don't start things off.

The "happy medium" is to begin your downswing from the ground up with the perfect timing of your hips, shoulders, arms, and hands. Doing anything else will only hurt your swing. For example:

- If your hips and legs jump out too far ahead of your arms, your shots will often slice off to the right.
- If you begin the downswing with the shoulders and arms (and not the lower body), you'll probably pull your ball to the left.
- If you combine a shoulder dive with slow forearms, you'll likely hit weak shots that first fly to the left and then slice back to the right (a pull-slice).
- If you practice until you swing with good timing, you'll be amazed at how long and straight your shots will fly!

◆ QUICK TIP ◆

It's common for the same thing to happen in baseball. To hit the ball to right field, the player (on the way through) leads with the lower body and lets the arms lag. To hit it to left field, the player leads more with the arms and less with the legs. To hit it to center field, just the right amount of body and arms needs to be blended into the swing.

my distance?" Everyone wants to hit the ball as far as possible—it's fun and can also lower your score. The secret? Create a powerful coil on the way back and swing with good timing.

The Backswing Coil—for More Distance

◖ On the way back, it's important to turn your shoulders about twice as far as your hips—with your back facing the target and your belt buckle pointing to your right shoe. This move energizes your swing, making it very powerful. It's much like twisting a flexible wire into a tight coil and then letting go to release all of the stored-up energy.

To do it right, here are two vital keys: First, load most of your weight on the inside edge of your back heel, not the outside. Second, keep your right leg in the same slightly bent position that it was when you addressed the ball. ◗

Swing with Good Timing—for More Distance

Ben Hogan described good timing as a "chain action," with the hips, shoulders, arms, and hands each starting to move just a split second ahead of the other as the downswing begins. Done right, the hips move first and send a multiplying power to the shoulders. In turn, the shoulders absorb this energy and conduct even more power to the arms. As the arms swing down toward the ball, still more power is transferred to the wrists. At last, the wrists unhinge and send the grand total of all energy down through your hands, the club, and into the ball. Surprisingly, a seemingly effortless swing builds enormous power, sending the ball much farther than you ever thought possible.

To get the chain action going, think of beginning the downswing from the ground up. This is known as the "magic move." Though one continuous move, here's the order things should happen:

1. Your lower body starts the downswing. Bump your hips a few inches toward your target—just enough to get your weight shifted from the back to the front foot. Turn your left side (left hip) out of the way as you keep swinging. Keep your left knee bent

get until you hit the ball.

2. Now feel the chain action work. Let the movements of your lower body cause your shoulders to unwind. The right elbow is pulled down to your right hip.

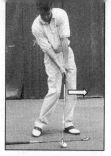

3. Finally, the chain action moves down into the arms. The forearms, wrists, and hands release the clubhead into the ball.

If any of these steps happen out of order, a major loss of power will result.

Be patient with yourself! It takes practice to get it right. Remember that there is an exact split-second schedule for each movement. The result is one "magic move." All good players begin their downswing from the ground up, starting with the lower body. That's why pros can swing so smoothly yet hit the ball so far!

> **♦ QUICK TIP ♦**
>
> As the magic move begins, keep your head back as you slide your hips forward to shift your weight to the front foot. So think: "bump hips forward—keep head back."

To Do It Right

When you swing . . .

On the Way Back

Turn back to target

Extend left arm

Keep right knee bent

Point left knee (behind ball) ➤

Weight loads on right heel
(on inside edge) ➤

Feel the coil

● Hips bump forward first
  (move left knee toward
  target)

  Shift weight forward
  (90 percent over left heel)

  Keep head back
  (until after impact)

● Roll forearms and
  wrists through

  Hear the swoosh
  (feel the speed!)

  Hold follow-through
  (hands over left
  shoulder)

✦ QUICK TIP ✦

On the way through, imagine swinging a long-handled broom.
The goal? Let your swing freewheel to build maximum power!

Common Goof-ups!

When you swing . . .

- ⃠ Don't sway off the ball and shift your weight to the outside of your back heel. ➡

- ⃠ Don't lift your left heel off the ground too much on the way back. ➡

- ⃠ Don't shift your weight to the front foot on the way back (a.k.a.: a reverse-weight shift). ➡

- ⃠ Don't grip too tightly during the downswing (which slows the forearm roll and wrist release, leading to slicing problems).

- ⃠ Don't leave your weight on your back foot as you swing through the ball.

Recap

- On the way back, load the weight on the inside of your right foot. Keep your right knee bent. Take a full shoulder turn.

- Begin the downswing with the "magic move." Lead with your hips and knees and let your arms drop into the "power slot."

- On the way through, shift 90 percent of your weight to your left foot.

- Finish the swing. Let the power of your swing carry you into a full follow-through.

> **JUST FOR FUN**
>
> "The greatest liar in the world is the golfer who claims he plays the game for merely exercise."
> —Tommy Bolt

What Now?

Go to Hole 12 and practice what you've learned.

12

LET'S PRACTICE!

If you find a drill that's really difficult for you, it probably means that's the drill you need the most.

—JIM FLICK

Full Swing

Are you ready to start hitting great golf shots? Practice the activities outlined in Steps 1, 2, and 3 and you'll be well on your way. The first step shows you how to swing freely and stay in perfect balance. Step 2 teaches you how to hit a hook by swinging your arms and hands properly on the way back and through. Step 3—where it really gets fun—gives you the inside scoop on how to hit the long ball!

1.   **Feet-Close-Together Swing.** Hit lots of practice shots with your feet close together (about four inches apart). Take a normal swing and move into a full follow-through. This drill helps prevent your body from swaying too much to the side and teaches you to keep your balance during the swing. You may even hit the ball better when you do this drill because it helps you to turn correctly and stay in good balance.

Hint: You have good swing balance when you can stay in your follow-through position indefinitely. After each of your swings, notice whether or not you can keep your balance.

The Goal: Swing your body in perfect balance.

2.   **Nonstop Swing.** Swing back and forth with only a brief pause between each complete swing. Do 10 to 20 nonstop quarter-, half-, and full-swings. Rest and repeat. This is a great drill that can help you swing smoothly and get the kinks out of your swing.

The Goal: Make your swing as "smooth as silk."

3. **Hear the Swoosh!** Take practice swings and notice if you can hear a loud swoosh sound on the way through. If you don't hear the swoosh at the bottom of the swing, pick up the pace and swing your body and arms faster!

4. **Feel the Speed.** Take 10 practice swings. On each swing, keep the speed on the way back about the same but gradually increase the speed on the way through. For instance, begin at about 10 percent of maximum speed on the way down, and then increase to about 20 percent on the next swing and so on until you reach 100 percent of maximum speed. At this point, back off to about 80 percent of your maximum speed and practice that swing. Hit a few shots at your best swing speed and see if you get good results.

The Goal: Find your ideal swing speed.

Step 2—Learn to Hit a Hook!

1. **9 o'clock Swing.** Use a short- or mid-iron and hit shots using a 9 o'clock swing. To do this drill, swing back until your left arm reaches 9 o'clock (or is level with the ground), and then change directions and swing down and through. Let the momentum of your swing carry your arms through to about 2 o'clock or so.

Occasionally, double-check that the toe of your club points to the sky on the way back.

On the way down, roll your forearms and release your wrists as fast as you can. This closes the clubface so your shot will curve to the left!

The Goal: Hit a hook on purpose.

> **◆ QUICK TIP ◆**
>
> Go with Harvey Penick's sage advice: "First you teach a golfer to hook the ball by using his hands and arms properly. Then you teach him how to take the hook away by using his body and legs properly."

Are you still looking for other good ways to free up your forearms and hit a hook? Try the following three drills.

Split-hands drill: Separate your hands so that they are about two or three inches apart on the clubshaft. Now hit a bucket of practice balls. Notice how this drill frees up your wrists and promotes an earlier forearm roll on the way down. ➤

Heavy-club drill: Swing with a weighted club. Sense how the extra weight encourages an earlier forearm roll.

Toe-in drill: Pull out a short- or mid-iron, address the ball, and take three swings. On the first two, swing back and pause when your hands reach shoulder height (about 10 o'clock), and then swing down slowly and stop just before the club

Clubface points left

gets to the ball. As you do this, make one simple adjustment: Turn your forearms (counterclockwise) well ahead of schedule so the toe of your clubface points in (faces left) before the club even reaches the ball. Do two "toe-in" practice swings and sense how it feels to roll your forearms early and ahead of schedule. Now take your stance and hit your ball. Try to roll your forearms early enough on the way down that you hit a hook—a shot that curves to the left—because the clubface is "toed-in" and pointing left as it comes into the ball.

1. **Magic Move.** Skip this drill until you can easily hit a hook shot on purpose. When you can, it's time to do the "magic move." As Harvey Penick suggests, the purpose of this drill is to take away your hook by teaching you how to use your hips and legs properly.

To do the magic move drill, swing to the top of your backswing, pause for a moment, and then begin your downswing by *slowly* bumping your hips several inches directly toward the target to shift your weight from your back to front foot. As this happens, let your arms swing down very *slowly* (just a foot or two) until your right elbow gently touches the side of your body. At this point, the end of the club should point slightly to the right of your target, with your wrists still fully hinged. (*Note:* Your shoulders begin to move automatically as you bump your hips forward.)

Now, swing the club back up to the top, pause, and repeat this *slow,* pumping motion one more time. Make

sure you feel connected, with the movement of your hips *causing* your right elbow to drop down to your right hip. Finally, address your ball and hit your shot. Notice how the swing feels when you lead with your hips and legs on the way down, and not with your arms or shoulders.

The pumping motion of this drill is like taking a short "check swing" in baseball. The arms are passive and are pulled down into the "power slot" simply by moving your hips to the left. As Ben Hogan put it, you should feel like your arms take a "free ride" until they are just about at hip level. After this, you'll be ready to quickly release your wrists and hands and swing your club through the hitting zone.

Note: When you do the magic move, make sure your hips bump a few inches directly toward the target and then turn out of the way. If the hips turn out of the way too fast (also called "spinning out"), you'll probably pull your shots to the left or hit a pull-slice. On the other hand, if the hips slide too far toward the target, you'll probably push or slice your shots off to the right.

❖ QUICK TIP ❖

Some top-notch golfers actually bump their hips (and shift their weight) toward the target a fraction of a second before their arms reach the top of the backswing. This is fine as long as the hips and legs initiate the downswing, and not the arms and hands.

The Goal: Learn the magic move! Let the arms drop down into the power slot as your hips bump to the left! (*Note:* You may find this drill a little challenging on the first few tries, so don't give up. Also, if this drill makes your slice worse, go back to the 9 o'clock drill until you can easily hit a hook on purpose.)

❯ QUICK TIP ❮

Here's a bonus power punch: Once you can do the magic move, don't be afraid to swing hard. In fact, Hogan said to hit the ball as hard as you can with both hands! It takes some practice to get to this point, but when you do—let it rip!

---

2. **Backswing Coil.** Crisscross your arms over your chest with a club pinned under your fingers. On the way back, turn your shoulders twice as far as your hips—with your back turned completely to the target and your hips turned so your belt buckle points to your right shoe. Also, load your weight on the inside of your back heel, but not the outside.

On the way through, move into a full follow-through. Shift 90 percent of your weight to your front foot with your belt buckle pointing to your target and your chest pointing to the left of the target.

The Goal: Energize your swing with a powerful coil. Go with Davis Love III's advice: "Turn your shoulders as much as you can [on the way back] while keeping your lower body quiet." Also, fine-tune the magic move as you practice this drill.

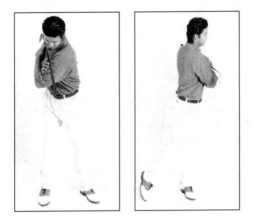

One More Thing

When you feel comfortable about doing the magic move, go to
the practice range and experiment a little. Notice how swinging
more with your arms and hands makes it easier to draw your
shots to the left, while using your hips and legs more (with the
arms lagging a little) causes your shots to fade to the right. Also
notice how bumping the hips correctly on the way down produces good shots while spinning out or sliding the hips too
much messes up your accuracy. Of course, the take-away mes-
sage is to learn how to synchronize your legs, hips, and arms
into a perfectly timed swing. You'll be glad you did!

✔ Quick Check

Show your instructor or partner your swing and ask for feedback. Jot down helpful hints you want to remember.

○	
○	
○	

137

"MUST-KNOW" SKILLS

13

I LOVE THE BEACH!

The sand shot ought to be the easiest shot in golf. You don't even have to hit the ball!

—WALTER HAGEN

Hey, I've Got a Question!

1. "What's the best way to hit a greenside bunker shot?"

Surprisingly, your club shouldn't even touch the ball! Instead, simply graze the top of the sand about two inches behind the ball as you swing through. The force of the swing splashes a handful of sand toward the target with your ball plopping out onto the green.

2. **"How should I swing when I hit from a greenside bunker?"** Other than hitting the sand instead of the ball, a greenside bunker shot is like any lob shot: Take a long, lazy swing, move your wrists freely, keep your arms and body relaxed, and make a full follow-through!

3. **"Is it worth the money to buy a sand wedge?"** Yes. A sand wedge is made to slide through the top surface of the sand and not dig in like other clubs. It's by far the best club to use for a greenside bunker and is also handy when hitting short (30- to 100-yard) pitch shots from the grass.

⚓ WORDS TO KNOW

Bunker: A part of the course where the turf has been removed and replaced with sand; also called a "sand trap."

Bounce: The wide, flanged bottom of a sand wedge. It keeps the club from digging deep into the sand.

Grounding the club: Touching your clubhead to the ground or sand before you swing.

Up and down: Hitting a chip or pitch shot from the grass (just off the green), and then taking one putt to hole your ball.

Sand save or "sandy": Hitting one shot from a greenside bunker and then taking one putt to hole your ball.

4. **"How do I hit a short versus long greenside bunker shot?"** Try the following adjustments:

For a shorter greenside bunker shot:

- Use a more lofted club (lob or sand wedge)
- Open up the clubface more (point it skyward)
- Take a more open stance
- Play the ball farther forward in your stance

For a longer greenside bunker shot:

- Use a less lofted club (pitching wedge or 9-iron)
- Keep the clubface squared or slightly open
- Take a square or slightly open stance
- Play the ball farther back in your stance

5. **"How is a fairway bunker shot different from a green-side bunker shot?"** When playing from a fairway bunker, hit the ball first, just like any other shot from the grass. Just

remember that a fairway bunker shot usually carries about ten yards less than the same shot from the fairway, so use a 6-iron from the sand if you normally hit a 7-iron off the fairway from that same distance.

6. **"I've got a bad lie in a sand bunker. How do I play it?"** Although it's easy to get overwhelmed, take courage from these helpful tips:

> **Buried or partially buried lie** (greenside *or* fairway bunker): Try using your pitching wedge instead of your sand wedge. Put your clubface in a square or closed position before taking your grip. Swing hard into the sand about two inches behind the ball. The ball will likely come out "hot" and roll a lot more than normal.
>
> **Wet or hard sand** (greenside bunker): Since the sand is firm and heavy, the clubface may bounce off the sand and directly into the ball. To stop this from happening, use a pitching wedge rather than a sand wedge, keep the clubface square instead of open (to help it dig into the sand), hit about two inches behind the ball, and make a full follow-through. For a fairway bunker shot, no adjustments are necessary.
>
> **Ball against the lip of the trap** (greenside *or* fairway bunker): Hit your shot out to the side or parallel to the lip. If your ball is buried deep into the lip, it may be best to take an unplayable lie penalty.

Wood play from the sand (fairway bunker): It takes lots of practice, but you can hit a fairway wood from the sand if you have a perfect lie and the lip of the bunker is level with the ball. To hit this shot: Open your clubface slightly to help prevent the club from digging in; aim a little to the left to compensate for  the open clubface; take a smooth, three-quarter-length swing; and hit the ball first as you sweep through the hitting zone.

7.   "**How can I put more backspin on my greenside bunker shot?**" If you're an advanced player, try to hit no more than an inch behind the ball, without touching the ball. Taking less sand increases the ball's spin rate and decreases roll when the ball hits the green. The challenge? If you catch too little sand and some ball, the shot will fly much farther than it should!

To Do It Right

When you take your stance (for a greenside bunker) . . .

Hold the club about an inch lower than normal for better control.

Fan your clubface open so it's facing skyward (before taking your grip). This helps the club splash through the sand and not dig in too much.

Play the ball slightly ahead of center, just inside of your left heel.

Open your stance (front foot is pulled back about six inches). Twist your feet down into the sand to improve your traction.

Look at a spot about two inches behind your ball since this is where you want your club to graze the sand (don't even look at the ball)!

Start with your hands a bit lower (closer to your legs). Also keep your hands even with the clubhead (don't slant your hands to the left).

Hold your clubface above the sand, about four inches away from the ball. *Hint:* It's a two-stroke penalty if you let your club touch the sand ("ground your club") when getting ready to hit any sand shot!

When your ball is on an up- or downhill slope, always set your shoulders and hips level with the slope before you swing. Then as you swing, let your club follow the slope of the sand.

When you swing . . .

On the Way Back

Wrists hinge smoothly

Long, lazy swing (swing to at least 9 o'clock)

Keep arms relaxed (fingers stay secure)

On the Way Through

Keep knees responsive

Splash sand forward

Swing through! (go well past 3 o'clock)

On the way down, don't worry about rolling your forearms to close the clubface. Rather, try to keep the clubface open and pointing to the sky as it skims through the sand.

Common Goof-ups!

When playing from a greenside bunker . . .

- ⊘ Don't begin the swing with your clubface squared (instead, open it so it points to the sky).

- ⊘ Don't ground your club when getting ready to hit any sand shot. (Two-stroke penalty.)

- ⊘ Don't hit too far behind the ball (or hit the ball first).

- ⊘ Don't take a long backswing and then stop too soon on the way through.

When you're in a greenside bunker (from a good lie):

- Before taking your grip, open your clubface so it points to the sky and open your stance to the target.

- Look directly at the sand as you take your swing. Hit about two inches behind the ball.

- Make a full follow-through.

When you're in a fairway bunker:

- Hit the ball first, just like any other normal shot.

What Now?

Go to Hole 14 and learn how to make great shots.

14

MAKE YOUR SHOT—
KEY TIPS

*A golfer learns something every time he hits the ball, and
he learns the most valuable lessons from the swings and
putts that don't work.*

—ARNOLD PALMER

Hey, I've Got a Question!

1. **"When am I supposed to take a divot?"** For short- and
midirons you should, but for longer irons, fairway woods,
and your driver, you shouldn't. Because a more level swing
is used with longer clubs, the club should brush the grass
when no tee is used, or leave the grass untouched when
driving from a tee.

If you take a divot, make sure you hit the ball first and then the ground—not the other way around (or your ball will never go as far as it should). Plus, just graze the top of the ground (don't dig too deep), and make sure your divot points toward your target. If you're having trouble, do the "feet-close-together" and "magic move" drills found on Hole 12.

2. **"My driver is so much harder to hit straight than my short irons. Why?"** Sidespin! Higher-lofted clubs put less sidespin (and more backspin) on the ball because the clubface hits near the bottom of the ball. The result is predictable: A high-flying shot with very little roll.

Your driver, on the other hand, has an almost flat-faced clubface so it hits much closer to the middle or equator of the ball and can add a lot more sidespin, as long as

the clubface is open or closed as the ball is hit. Depending on the clubface position at impact, the ball will spin off to the right or off to the left. Of course, it is possible to hit a straight drive; it's just a lot harder to do!

♦ QUICK TIP ♦

Is it easier to hook your ball around a tree with a 3-iron or a 5-iron? The 3-iron, because it has a flatter face and hits a bit closer to the equator of the ball, producing more sidespin (when the face is closed) than backspin.

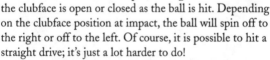

3.   "I have a hard time hitting my fairway woods and long irons. Any advice?" Yes, here are three tips: First, play the ball a little forward (about even with your left heel) and swing level with the ground to sweep the ball from the grass. Second, let the loft of the clubface do what it's supposed to do—lift your ball up into the air. Don't let your body dip down in an attempt to get your ball airborne. Take a smooth, sweeping swing. Third, practice! Soon, you'll enjoy hitting a 3-iron almost as much as a 9-iron!

4.   "Why do my full shots fly to the right or to the left? What can I do to be more accurate?" There are two main things that determine the direction of your shots: The path of the club as it comes into the ball and the angle of the clubface at impact. The club's path as it hits into the ball

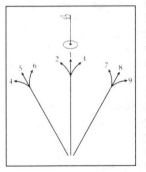

sets the initial direction the ball will fly, while the clubface angle mostly determines whether your shot will curve as it flies through the air.

Now, with these two things in mind, there are nine different flight patterns your shot could travel after you hit the ball. It could fly straight, be pulled to the left with a curve to the right, be pushed to the right with a curve to the left, and so on. You will improve your accuracy if you understand the cause of each ball-flight pattern. Studying these causes will make it a lot easier to find your exact swing error and know what to do to fix it.

fixing them:

Slice: a shot that curves from left to right

> **What causes it:** The clubface is open as it hits the ball.
>
> **Possible goof-ups:** • Gripping with the V's not pointing to your right shoulder. • Fanning the clubface open too far on the way back. • Swinging the arms up too steeply on the way back. • Not closing the clubface fast enough on the way down. • Swinging out of sync on the way down—with your hips racing too far ahead and your arms lagging too far behind.
>
> **How to fix it:** • Get some good instruction. Hit 100+ balls doing the 9 o'clock swing drill. • Turn your left knuckles under a little on the way back (make sure the toe of your club points to the sky on the way back). • Speed up your forearm roll on the way through. • Think more about your arms as you swing (until you straighten out the slice). Do the split-hands, heavy club, and toe-in drills. • Relax and make a loud swoosh on the way through!

◆ QUICK TIP ◆

It's a lot harder to fix a slice when you're using a long iron or one of your woods. A better way to go is to drop down to a 7-iron and practice the 9 o'clock swing drill. When it's easy to hook your 7-iron, see if you can do the same with your longer clubs and a longer swing.

151

Pull-Slice: a shot that starts left and then curves back to the right

> **What causes it:** The club swings across the ball along an out-to-in path (this sends the ball to the left). At the same time, the clubface is open as it hits the ball (which slices the ball back to the right).

> **Possible goof-ups:** • Standing too close to the ball. • Starting the downswing with your shoulders and arms (a shoulder dive) instead of your hips. • Turning the hips out of the way too fast. • Not rolling the forearms fast enough. • Rushing the change in direction on the way back and forth.

> **How to fix it:** • To fix the pull—do the "magic move" drill before every shot. • Start each downswing from the ground up, by bumping the hips forward and shifting your weight! This pulls your arms into the "power slot," which moves the clubhead on an inside path to the ball, instead of coming over the top. • Slow down the transition on the way back and forth. Say "one AND two" to help pace your swing. • To fix the slice—follow the tips given above.

Push: a shot that flies straight, but to the right

> **What causes it:** The club swings through the ball (with a square clubface) along an in-to-out path.

> **Possible goof-ups:** • Standing too far from the ball. • Aiming to the right of your target (pointing your stance

parallel-left). • Playing the ball too far back in your stance. • Not turning your body enough on the way through (so your belt buckle points to the right of your target by the time you finish the swing).

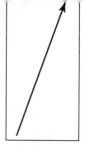

How to fix it: • Perfect your posture, ball position, and aim. • Learn to turn on the way through so your belt buckle, belly button, and chest all point to the left of your target when you finish.

Hook: a shot that curves from right to left

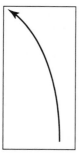

What causes it: The clubface is closed as it hits the ball.

Possible goof-ups: • Closing the clubface on the way back by bowing your left wrist. • Spinning the clubface into the ball too fast on the way down. • Not doing the magic move right.

How to fix it: • Get some good instruction. Hit 100+ balls doing the magic move drill. • Bump your hips toward the target to begin the downswing. • Make sure the toe of your club points to the sky on the way back. • Turn your shoulders fully on the way back. • Don't try to hit your shot as far as possible! • Think more about your hips and legs as you swing (until you straighten out the hook).

Mis-hits: scooping (hitting too far behind ball), also called a "fat" shot, or topping (hitting the top or middle of the ball), also called a "thin" shot

What causes it: The body sways to the side or bobs up and down during the swing.

Possible goof-ups: • Bending your left arm too much on the way back • A poor coil or weight shift on the way back. • Straightening out the knees or spine on the way back. • Bending more at the knees or hips on the way down. • Failing to shift your weight to the left foot on the way through.

How to fix it: • Get some good instruction. Hit 100+ balls with your feet close together. • Practice the "backswing coil" (Hole 12). • Keep your head level. • Make a full shoulder turn while loading the weight on the inside of your right foot. • Learn to shift your weight correctly as your body turns during your swing—without swaying.

◆ QUICK TIP ◆

If you have the problem of swaying during your swing, remember this tip from Percy Boomer: Imagine a wooden barrel around your midsection, with just a couple of inches between its sides and your hips. As you swing, think of moving inside the barrel without touching the sides!

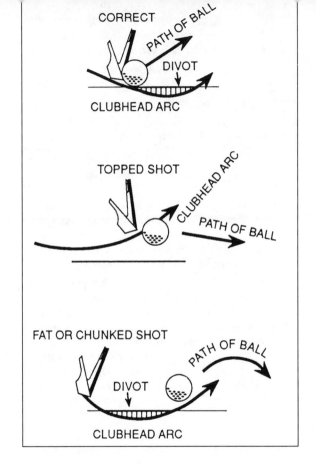

CORRECT

PATH OF BALL

DIVOT

CLUBHEAD ARC

TOPPED SHOT

CLUBHEAD ARC

PATH OF BALL

FAT OR CHUNKED SHOT

DIVOT

PATH OF BALL

CLUBHEAD ARC

Low Power

What causes it: Slow clubhead speed or an open club-face as the ball is hit.

Possible goof-ups:
• Swinging the club too slow because of weak muscles. • Bending your left arm too much on the

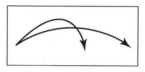

way back. • Not coiling your shoulders or shifting your weight correctly. • Swinging too much with your arms. Not doing the "magic move." • Failing to swing into a full follow-through. • Hitting a slice, which results in high, weak shots.

How to fix it: • Practice the swoosh, nonstop, toe-in, 9 o'clock, magic move, coil, and feet-close-together drills.
• Create maximum power by doing the magic move correctly—with the perfect timing of the legs, hips,

---

⛳ WORDS TO KNOW

Toed shot: Hitting the ball off the toe of the clubface.

Heeled shot: Hitting the ball off the heel of the clubface (near the neck or hosel of the clubshaft).

Topped shot: Hitting the middle or "top" of the ball; also called a thin or sculled shot.

Fat shot: Hitting the turf before the ball.

Shank: Hitting the ball off the hosel of the club—leading to a shot that veers sharply to the right.

When everything else is the same, a pull to the left usually goes the farthest, since the ball is hit flush as the clubhead swings across it on an out-to-in pathway. This is a "hot" shot

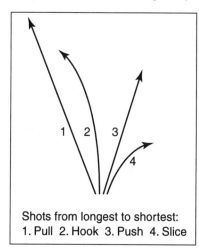

Shots from longest to shortest:
1. Pull 2. Hook 3. Push 4. Slice

that flies straight (left of the target), a little lower than normal, and usually gets a lot of roll and oftentimes finds trouble. A hook goes almost as far, but because it curves to the left instead of flying straight, it doesn't go quite as far. A push to the right is in the middle of the mix and doesn't go quite as far as a hook. The weakest of the four shots is the slice, because the clubface is open (which increases clubface loft), so the ball not only flies high but curves to the right at the same time.

> **Did You Know?** The amount of curve to the right when the clubface is open by only one degree (one degree out of a 360-degree circle) at the point of impact, on a 200-yard shot hit by your driver: 10 yards!

6. "How can I hit a high shot over a tree or low shot into the wind?"

The High Shot (over a tree)

• Use a higher-lofted club; open the clubface a little before taking your grip. • Take an open stance with slightly more weight on your right foot, at address.

• Play the ball forward in your stance— an inch or so more than normal. Set your hands even with or slightly behind the ball. • Aim a little to the left to make up for the open clubface.
• Exaggerate the finish. Swing your hands and arms as high as possible on the way through.

◆ QUICK TIP ◆

To hit a nice, high shot, it helps to have a thin cushion of grass directly under your ball. This lets your club easily slide under and hit the bottom half of the ball.

The Low Shot (to keep your ball down out of the wind)

• Use a less lofted club and close the clubface a little before taking your grip. • Take a square stance with slightly more weight on your front foot. • Play the ball back in your stance—an inch or so more than normal. • Slant your hands to the left, well ahead of the ball. • Aim a little to the right to make up for the closed clubface. • Limit your wrist action on the way back and through. • Abbreviate the finish. Swing your hands, arms, and club as low as possible on the way through. Keep your arms low and fully extended as you finish the swing.

7. "How can I shape my shots so they curve to the right or to the left?"

The Draw (a slight curve from right to left)

• Aim a little to the right, so your swing pathway initially hits the ball to the right of your target. • Before taking your grip, close the clubface just enough to draw your ball back to your target.
• Swing smooth and trust your swing.

The Fade (a slight curve from left to right)

• Aim a little to the left, so your swing pathway initially hits the ball to the left of your intended target. • Before taking your grip, open the clubface just enough to slice or fade your ball back to your target.

• Swing smooth and trust your swing.

> **◆ QUICK TIP ◆**
>
> What's explained above is one way to shape your shots. You can also speed up your forearm roll on the way down (to hit a draw) or pay more attention to your hips and legs (to hit a fade). Most importantly, use the approach that works best for you and your swing.

8. **"If I have to hit a shot from uneven ground, should I do anything differently?"** Your ball tends to fly in the same direction that the ground is sloping. For example, if you are standing on a side hill with the ball above your feet, your shot tends to move a little to the left—in the same direction the ground is slanting. The opposite is true with the ball below your feet—the ball tends to fly to the right.

A down- or uphill lie affects both the direction and the distance of the shot. For instance, a ball hit from a downhill lie tends to travel farther because it flies lower and rolls more. This kind of shot also tends to fly right. The opposite is true for an uphill lie: the ball doesn't go as far because it flies higher and moves more to the left.

When you are on uneven ground, take several practice swings to get a feel for the lie. Notice where your club first brushes the grass; this can help you know where to position your stance across from the ball.

The Uphill Shot

• Use more club than normal (a 7-iron instead of an 8-iron) • Play the ball forward in your stance, closer to the higher or front foot. • Set your shoulders and hips level with the slope. • Grip down on the club a little. • Aim a little to the right (since the ball tends to fly left). • Take only a ³/₄-length backswing to help you keep your balance.

The Downhill Shot

• Use less club than usual (an 8-iron instead of a 7-iron). • Play the ball back in your stance, closer to the higher (back) foot. • Set your shoulders and hips parallel to the slope. • Aim a little to the left (since the ball tends to fly right). • Take only a ³/₄-length backswing, so you can stay in perfect balance.

The Side Hill Shot—Ball above Your Feet

• Stand a little farther from the ball to help you stand taller. Put slightly more weight toward your toes. • Grip down on the club several inches, so your arms extend to a normal length. • Aim farther right than usual. • Take a $^3/_4$-length backswing so you can keep your balance. Sweep the ball off the turf without taking a divot.

The Side Hill Shot—Ball below Your Feet

• Stand a little closer to the ball, bend more from the hips and knees, put more weight on your heels, and get into a low "sit-down" position so you can reach the ball. • Grip up on the club a little so your arms stay extended. • Aim a little to the left and take a $^3/_4$-length backswing. • Keep your head steady. Swing in balance.

Common Goof-ups!

When making your shot . . .

- 🚫 Don't hit behind the ball. Instead hit the ball first, and then the turf.
- 🚫 Don't try to get the ball airborne by changing your swing.
- 🚫 Don't change your swing (instead, keep it the same as your practice swings).
- 🚫 Don't lose your balance.
- 🚫 Don't try to hit impossible shots from uneven lies.

Recap

- A slice goes high and short; a hook goes long and low.
- Every golfer should learn to hit a draw, fade, low shot, and high shot.
- When you hit from uneven lies—adjust your stance, posture, ball position, and swing.

What Now?

Go to Hole 15 and learn how to play smart.

JUST FOR FUN

"The fact that trees are 90% air does not mean your ball will avoid the remaining 10% of timber."

—golfjokes.co.uk 🏌

PLAY SMART—FIND
YOUR GAME!

Most golfers prepare for disaster. A good golfer prepares
for success.

—BOB TOSKI

Hey, I've Got a Question!

1. **"Should I buy new or used clubs?"** Usually you can get
the most for your money if you buy top-quality, used equipment. Every once in a while you can find a great deal on
new clubs. It all depends on your preferences and timing.
Golf course pro shops, local golf stores, Internet golf sites,
and wholesale golf outlets offer an array of both new and
used equipment. Shop around.

Before buying any clubs, ask an expert to help you pick out clubs that fit your body size and strength. For example, he or she should make sure that the club's lie angle, length, loft, shaft flex, shaft material, grip size, grip material,

and swing weight are right for you. (See Hole 18 for more information on this.) Whenever possible, try out a "demo set" (of the clubs you hope to buy) on the course to see if you like the way they look and how they perform.

2. "Does it matter what type of ball I use?" Golf balls tend to fall into two categories—good and excellent. The "good" ones are less expensive, have cut-proof covers, and give you good distance, but they usually have a hard and bouncy feel when you hit them. Common brand names in this category include Pinnacle, Dunlop, and certain Top Flight balls. Beginners and many intermediate players like these balls because the price is right and the lower quality isn't that noticeable.

The "best" balls feel good when you hit them, give you excellent distance, and produce a high spin rate (so they stop sooner after they land on the green), but they may be less durable since they sometimes scratch and cut easier. Common brands include Titleist, Top Flight, Callaway, and Nike, to name a few.

3. **"Do you have any tips for playing in stormy weather?"**
Yes, follow these commonsense suggestions:

Playing in the rain: Go
with more club (a 4-iron
instead of a 5-iron) when
the ground is soft and
moist. Carry a fiberglass
umbrella, a dry towel, and
lightweight rainwear in
your golf bag. Hook the
dry towel to the inside of
your umbrella so moisture
can be easily removed
from your hands and club

grips before each shot. Wear a glove and good golf
shoes to prevent slipping.

Playing in the heat: Use less club (a 7-iron instead of
a 6-iron) when the ground is dry and hard. Wear lightweight and light-colored clothing. Wear a hat or visor
to shade your eyes, use sunscreen, and drink plenty
of water. Consider using a riding cart (with a canopy)
when it's extremely hot, or wait until a cooler time of
day to play.

Playing in the cold: Go with more club because your
ball won't fly as far. Wear layered clothing so you can
remove or add layers as needed. If it's really cold, wear
a knit hat to cover your ears and head. Wear mittens
between shots to keep your hands warm.

For every 10 mph increase in headwind, play one extra club (8-iron instead of a 9-iron). Do the opposite for a tailwind.

Playing in the wind: The wind has a big effect on where your ball ends up. If you play into a strong headwind, you may need to hit much more club (a 4-iron instead of a 7-iron). The opposite is true when playing downwind. A cross- or headwind is also tricky because it adds sidespin to your ball, making it slice or hook much more than normal. When it's windy, it's hard to keep your balance, so use a wider stance than normal, take no more than a ³/₄-length backswing, and swing easy!

4. **"What should I do if I find my ball in these situations?"**

  • **Ball in deep, tangled grass:** To cut through to the ball, use a short- or mid-iron. Square the clubface to your intended aim line, play the ball back in your stance a little, grip the club firmly, hinge your wrists freely on the way back and through, and swing steeply into the grass, just behind the ball.

  • **Ball in a divot:** Since you need to dig down into the turf to get your ball out, use a short- or mid-iron, play the ball back in your stance, and swing aggressively through the hitting zone. Practice this shot on the driving range so you know what to expect.

- **Ball on bare, hard ground:** Concentrate on hitting the lower half of the ball first, just like you would on a fairway bunker shot. Try to clip the ball right off.
- **Ball blocked by a tree:** Consider your options. Go with the safest bet; if possible, hit under, around, or over the tree. This is one time when knowing how to hit a draw, fade, low, and high shot can come in handy!
- **Ball in shallow water:** Try this shot only when part of your ball is above the water line. Use a short iron, square the clubface to your intended aim line, look at a point about two inches behind the ball, and hit forcefully down and through the hitting zone. You might also want to take off your shoes and wear a rain suit!

When you're in trouble, take your medicine and get your ball back to the friendly fairway as soon as possible. Trying to be a hero usually just makes things worse.

5. **"When I hit my ball from light rough, it goes farther than I expect it to. Why's that?"** This happens when the clubface and ball are unable to make direct contact. For example, if a thin layer of grass covers the clubface at impact, it will decrease backspin, making your ball fly lower and farther, and roll more after landing. If you think you have a so-called "flyer" lie, drop back a club or two (from a 5- to a 6-iron) to compensate for the effect. Remember that wet grass magnifies the problem, so take this into account as well.

6.   "How come my practice swing feels so good, but my actual swing feels so bad?!" When the stakes are low, so is your muscle tension. It's easy to swing smooth and stay relaxed when nothing is on the line. As you take your actual swing, though, your muscles may tighten up so much that it totally changes your swing. Surprisingly, a happy medium provides the best results. A little nervousness is good—it helps you think and perform better. So don't try to silence the pressure completely, just learn to control it!

7.   "How can I play smart without making dumb mistakes?!" Johnny Miller said, "It is always the player who takes the most into consideration who comes up a winner." It's true. There's so much to think about and so many decisions to make when you're out golfing. If you play smart, you'll save yourself a lot of strokes. How's it done? First, remember that experience is the best teacher of all. Learn from your mistakes.
Second, be patient and enjoy the challenge. No one can master this game! If you hit a bad shot or make a dumb mistake, it's no big deal. Be positive and make it right the next time around! Third, follow the tips outlined on the next few pages.

> ♦ **QUICK TIP** ♦
>
> After you take a practice swing or two, address your ball and go on autopilot. Swing like a machine! Keep your expectations exactly the same. Relax, trust your swing, and let it freewheel!

To Do It Right

When you get ready to play . . .

Check in. Try to get to the course about 30 minutes before your tee time. Stop by the starter's desk and pay your green fees. Also, pick up a scorecard and pencil and make sure you have a ball marker or coin, plenty of tees, and at least six balls in your bag.

Slowly swing two clubs

Warm up and stretch. Go to the practice range and stretch for several minutes. Finish up by holding two irons in your hands and swinging them back and forth for a minute or two.

Hint: If you have the time and money, it's a good idea to hit a small bucket of practice range balls (available from the pro shop) before you go play. (Note: Range balls can be used on the practice range and putting greens, but not out on the course.)

Hit practice balls. If you decide to hit range balls, first take out one of your short irons and hit 15 to 20 shots with a 9 o'clock (or half-) swing. Get a feel for your swing. Now, lengthen your swing and hit four or five shots with a 9-iron, 7-iron, 5-iron, 3-iron, 3-wood, and driver. Aim for a specific target on each shot.

Chipping warm-up. Go to the practice green and hit a few chip shots to specific targets. Get a feel for the speed of the greens.

Hint: Most courses let you use their practice putting greens for free. If you're short on time and can't play nine holes, spend a little time on a practice green and tune up your short game.

Hint: Keep in mind that the speed of the greens can vary considerably from one course to another.

Putting warm-up. Hit both long and short putts. Just before your tee-time, make a few short putts to build your confidence.

When you play the game . . .

Keep things simple. As you swing, think only about your target and what you wish to accomplish. If you have a single swing thought that works, go ahead and use it.

Play each shot, one at a time. Think only of your current challenge and what you want to do. Good players don't dwell on previous mistakes or the final score.

Know your distances. Before each approach shot, look for distance markers placed along the hole. These tell you how far you need to hit your ball to reach the green.

Keep your equipment clean. Some players like to carry a damp towel on their golf bag. It's a handy way to clean your club after each shot, and your ball after reaching the green.

Hit your ball away from trouble. If there's a hazard on the left side of the fairway, hit your ball to the right side away from the trouble (or vice versa). Always give yourself a margin of error in case you hit your ball a little off-line.

Play for the best angles. If the cup is on the left side of the green, hit your drive to the right side of the fairway (or vice versa); this gives you a better angle to hit your approach shot into the green.

It's not a "long-drive" contest! Don't always try to hit your tee shots as far as possible. Instead, decide how many yards you want your second shot to be, imagine a spot where your ball should land, and then use the right club from the tee to give you the desired distance left to the green.

Don't push your luck. If there's trouble over the green, like a water hazard or a sand bunker, use less club and hit your shot a little short of the cup instead of beyond it. If the cup happens to be close to a greenside bunker (sometimes called a "sucker pin"), give yourself a margin of error and hit to the middle of the green instead.

Stay energized. Drink plenty of water and take along a few snacks, such as an energy bar, raisins, or an apple, to keep your energy levels high.

Be polite! Walk fast between shots so others don't have to wait for you. Replace all of your divots on the fairway; fix all of your ball marks on the green.

Keep score and have fun. Play by the rules and keep score so you can track your progress.

Enjoy the walk! Don't use a cart unless you have to. Walk the course whenever you can. It's a true golfing tradition!

Common Goof-ups!

When you play...

- ⊘ Don't arrive so late to the course that you don't have time to warm up.

- ⊘ Golf's tough enough already. Don't forget to follow the smart playing tips you know about.

- ⊘ Don't take unnecessary risks. Play the best percentage shot and stay out of trouble.

- ⊘ Don't dwell on past mistakes. Always remember your best shots.

Recap

- Arrive at the course with plenty of time to spare. Check in, stretch, hit a few practice shots, and get to the first tee before your tee time.

> **JUST FOR FUN**
>
> Golf is a game in which the slowest people in the world are those in front of you, and the fastest are those behind. 🏌

- Play smart. Know your distances. Keep your equipment clean. Don't push your luck. Be polite. Enjoy the walk.

What Now?

Go to Hole 16 and practice what you've learned.

16

LET'S PRACTICE!

Practice must be interesting, even absorbing, if it is to be of any use.

—BOBBY JONES

Sand Play

1. **Hit the Line.** Draw a long, straight line in the sand with the end of your club (the line should point away from you). Place your ball just in front of the line. Now take your shot and see if you can skim your clubhead into the sand right on the line.

Hint: When you play from the sand, never touch (or "ground") your club to the sand before taking your swing or it's a two-stroke penalty. It's fine to take a couple of practice swings above the sand—just don't hit the sand before the actual shot.

The Goal: Swing the club through the sand at the right place.

2. **Splash it Out!** Use the end of your club and draw a small box around your ball. On each shot, think of splashing the sand out of the box to loft your ball up and out of the bunker.

3. **Cluster Drill.** Get a small bucket of balls. Hit short, medium, and long greenside bunker shots by adjusting your ball position and clubface angle, and changing the length of your swing. Try to cluster the balls into three groups (about 15 feet apart).

Intermediate drill: Plop five balls down in a greenside bunker. Hit five shots from short to long, with each shot going about five to ten feet farther than the previous shot.

Special Shots

1. **Fades, Draws, High and Low Shots.** Go to the practice range and hit at least 10 balls for each shot (fades, draws, high shots, and low shots).

2. **Uneven Lies.** Find a place off to the side of the practice putting green or driving range to hit uphill, downhill, and side hill shots. Take about 10 practice swings to get a feel for the shot and to identify the bottom of your swing; then hit several shots with wiffle balls.

of shot. You earn one point when you hit the best shot (from a divot or thick rough, lob shots, sand shots, fade or draw around an obstacle, high and low shots, and so on). The first player to earn seven points wins.

Smart Golf

1. **Welcome to the Course!** Here's a checklist to remind you how to get ready for your round of golf.

✔	What to Do
	Check in. If possible, get to the course about 30 minutes before your tee-time. Pick up a scorecard and a pencil. Make sure you have a ball marker or coin, plenty of tees, and at least a half-dozen balls in your bag.
	Warm up and stretch. Tune up your body so you're in touch with your swing.
	Hit practice balls. Start with about 20 half-swing shots to get a feel for your swing. After this, hit several full-swing shots with your 9-iron, 7-iron, 5-iron, 3-iron, 3-wood, and driver.
	Chipping warm-up. Hit a few long and short chip shots to different targets.
	Putting warm-up. Hit some long and short putts. Go to the first tee with several minutes to spare.

2. **It's Time to Play!** Here's a checklist to remind you how to play smart:

✔	What to Do
	Keep things simple. Don't fill your mind with a bunch of swing thoughts. Think only about your target and what you wish to accomplish. Go ahead and use a single swing thought if it helps you play better.
	Play each shot, one at a time. Think only of your current challenge and what you want to do.
	Know your distances. Before each shot, know the exact distance you need to hit your ball.
	Keep your equipment clean. If you'd like, use a damp towel to clean your club after each shot, and your ball after reaching the green.
	Hit your ball away from trouble. If there's a hazard on the left side of the fairway, hit your ball to the right side, away from the trouble (or vice versa).
	Play for the best angles. If the cup is on the left side of the green, hit your drive to the right side of the fairway (or vice versa).
	Don't push your luck. Play smart and don't take unnecessary risks.
	Stay energized. Drink plenty of water and take along an energy bar or an apple, to boost your energy levels.

✔	**What to Do** (*continued*)
	Be polite! Play fast. Replace your divots. Fix any ball marks on the green.
	Keep score and have fun. Play by the rules, keep score, and enjoy your round.
	Enjoy the walk! Walk the course whenever you can—it's a great form of exercise!

✔ Quick Check

Show your instructor or partner your swing and ask for feedback. Also, discuss the strengths and weaknesses of your current golf game. Jot down helpful hints you want to remember:

RULES, LOGS,
AND MORE

GOLF RULES
MADE SIMPLE

*All of us who opt to use the Rules of Golf in competitions
and in everyday golf do so because we respect the USGA
and R&A and because we recognize that uniformity in
golf is eminently desirable. The game is more enjoyable if
we all play the same game.*

—TOM WATSON

Hey, I've Got a Question!

1. **"I've heard there are two kinds of competitions—
stroke play and match play. What's the difference?"** Stroke
play is a game where the person who shoots the lowest total
score after 18 or more holes wins. Most professional tournaments are stroke-play events and last four days (with

major stroke-play championships include The Masters, U.S. Open, British Open, and PGA Championship.

Match play is a fun hole-by-hole competition. The player with the lowest score on each hole earns one point (or in the case of ties, each player earns a half-point). At the end of the match, the player (or team) with the most points (or holes) wins. An exciting match-play championship is The Ryder Cup, where the top players from the United States and United Kingdom compete head-to-head.

Note: To keep things simple, the rules in this lesson apply only to stroke play. Penalties for match play are similar but usually lead to the loss of the hole (or point) rather than a one- or two-stroke penalty.

2. **"How about if a rule tells me to drop the ball? What do I do?"** Face any direction, hold your ball level with your shoulder, keep your arm straight, and then drop it either in front of or to the side of you. The drop is good when your ball stops no nearer to the hole than it was before you dropped it and the right distance away from the problem area.

"How do I know what the right distance is?" It depends on whether you are being penalized or not. If it's a no-penalty or free drop situation, drop your ball no more than one club-length away from the problem area (or take the nearest relief).

If you are being penalized, drop your ball no more than two club-lengths away from the hazard line or problem area (or follow the specific rule).

"Do I sometimes need to drop again?" Yes, re-drop your ball if it bounces off the ground and hits you or your equipment. (Re-drop as many times as needed without penalty.) Drop your ball again if it lands and rolls nearer to the hole, more than two club-lengths away from where it first struck a part of the course, out of bounds, onto a putting green, back into a hazard, or out of a sand trap (that it should stay in). If the second drop is still not a good one, pick up your ball and place it where it first struck a part of the course. (No penalty.)

◆ QUICK TIP ◆

How you drop your ball depends on where your last shot was taken from. For example, if you were on:

- A tee box—Re-tee or place your ball for your next stroke (your choice).
- The green—Place your ball for your next stroke.
- Anywhere else—Drop or place your ball for your next shot (do what the specific rule tells you to do).

Sometimes you can take a free drop with no penalty. When? If you find that your ball, stance, or swing is in, on, or affected by any of the following:

1. Casual water (this is any temporary puddle that's not in a water hazard but is visible before or after you take your stance).
2. Ground under repair (usually marked with lines drawn along the ground).
3. A hole made by a burrowing animal.
4. The droppings from an animal (but not from the footprint of an animal or bird).
5. A cart path or road (at the point of nearest relief; no nearer the hole).
6. A green that's for another hole or any practice green.
7. A stake or wire that supports a young tree, ball washer, drinking fountain, sprinkler head (or other immovable artificial obstructions), but not from a hazard stake or out-of-bounds fence.
8. A plugged or embedded lie where your ball is stuck down in soft turf (as long as the grass is cut to the length of the fairway or shorter).

For numbers 1 through 7, drop your ball within one club-length from its original spot (or nearest relief) but no nearer the hole. For number 8, drop your ball as close as possible to the original spot but no nearer the hole.

Does This Count as a Penalty?

Not every little thing you do out on the course costs you a penalty. Here are a few examples of things you can get away with:

1. You can re-tee your ball if it happens to fall off the tee or is bumped off by your club (before your first swing).
2. You can clean your ball when you mark and pick it up from the putting green, take a penalty drop or free drop, or walk from one hole to the next.
3. It's fine if your shot hits the flagstick or another ball on the green when you're hitting from off the green. Play your ball as it lies, and if you've hit an opponent's ball, take it back to its original spot.
4. You can fix any ball mark on the green at any time (but don't fix spike marks until after you've finished the hole).
5. It's fine to move a twig, loose stone, or pinecone (loose natural impedi-
ments) away from
your ball at any time,
except when your ball
is in a sand bunker or
water hazard.

6.   It's okay to move a paper cup, cigarette butt, rake, or hose (movable artificial obstructions) away from your ball at any time, in or out of a hazard.

7.   You can talk about anything with your opponent that's common knowledge, such as the distance of a given hole or where on-course distance markers are posted, but you can't give or ask your opponent for advice (the penalty for this is explained in #27 in the next section).

Now I'm in Trouble! Any Advice?

Here are some of the most common rules and penalties that you need to know about:

1.   **"Whoops, I just hit from in front of the tee markers!"** Add two strokes to your score, and then hit again from the right place. Where's that? Anywhere between the tee markers (not in front of them), and not more than two club-lengths behind the *front* edge of the markers. (Don't count your first stroke; just add a two-stroke penalty to your score.)

♣ WORDS TO KNOW

Loose natural impediments: Any natural object (such as stones, pinecones, leaves, or twigs) that's not growing from or firmly fixed to the ground.

Movable artificial obstructions: Any manmade object (such as rakes, litter, or hoses) that can easily be moved away from your ball or stance.

---

2. **"My ball just said 'see ya' and flew out of bounds!"** If your ball "waves goodbye" and leaves the course (marked by a fence, a white line, or white stakes), it's a one-stroke penalty. To put another ball into play, hit again from as close as possible to where your original shot was last played and add two strokes to your score—one for the initial stroke and one for penalty. Ouch! Remember you can re-tee your ball if the original shot was from the tee box.

If it turns out that your original ball is still in bounds, you can play it and pick up the provisional ball. (No penalty.) If your original ball is out (or if you didn't do the first and second steps correctly), add two strokes to your score and play your provisional ball.

◆» QUICK TIP ◆◄

If you believe your ball is out of bounds, always hit a "provisional" shot *before* going to look for your ball. (This will save you from having to go back to the original spot.) When you do, follow two steps:

- First, tell the other players in your group that you're going to play a provisional shot (*before* you hit it and *before* you look for your original ball).
- Second, play your provisional ball *after* all other players in your group have played their first shots.

3. **"My ball's lost! Now what?"** The penalty for losing your ball is the same as hitting it out of bounds, so you'll have to take the same medicine; hit again from as close as possible to where you played your original shot and add two strokes to your score—one for the initial stroke and one for the penalty. You should hit a provisional ball before going forward if you believe your ball will be hard to find.

"When is my ball lost?" Whenever you:

- Don't identify it within five minutes after you begin looking for it, or
- Put another ball into play (by either dropping, placing, or teeing a second ball).

♦ QUICK TIP ♦

These last two rules are called "stroke and distance" penalties because you count the first stroke that led to the problem along with a penalty stroke, and you have to go back to the original place where the ball was played (distance penalty).

---

4. **"My ball flew into the lake in front of the green!"** It's important to know that a water hazard is a lake or stream located between the hole's teeing area and the green (it is marked with yellow stakes or a yellow line drawn along the ground). If your ball lands in a water hazard, you've got three options:

Splash!

a. Play your ball as it lies if it is along the shoreline or is in very shallow water, but don't touch your club to the ground before you swing. (No penalty.)

b. Drop the ball from as far behind the hazard as you would like, keeping the point at which your original ball *last* flew, bounced, or rolled over the hazard line directly between your drop point and the flagstick. (One penalty stroke.) Got that? Try reading this again, but this time, visualize it in your mind's eye. Notice how these three points (the drop point, the place where the ball crossed the hazard line, and the flagstick) all form a straight line.

c. Go back and play another ball as close as possible to the point from which the original ball was last played. (One penalty stroke.)

5. **"My ball bounced into the stream alongside the fairway!"** This is called a lateral water hazard (because the water is along the side of the hole and is marked with red stakes or a red line). If your ball lands in a lateral water hazard, you can

go with one of the three water-hazard options above or choose from two more one-stroke penalty options:

    a. Drop your ball within two club-lengths from where your original ball *last* crossed the hazard line but no nearer to the hole.

    b. Drop your ball within two club-lengths on the other side of the hazard (opposite from where your original ball last crossed the hazard line) but no nearer to the hole.

◆ QUICK TIP ◆

If you think your shot might have gone into a water hazard, you're not allowed to hit a provisional shot before going forward to look for your ball. What can you do? Try to find your ball. If it's in the water, choose your best option and go from there.

---

6. **"My ball is under a tree! I can't even get a club on it. Now what?"** If your ball is in any position (except in a water hazard) that you think is not playable, you can pick it up, clean it, give yourself a one-stroke penalty, and choose from one of three options:

    a. Drop within two club-lengths from where your unplayable ball was found but no nearer to the hole.

    b. Drop your ball as far behind your original lie as you would like, keeping your drop point, original lie, and the flagstick in a straight line. (One penalty stroke.)

c. Get as close as possible to the spot where your original ball was last played, and drop or tee-up another ball.

> ◆ **QUICK TIP** ◆
>
> If you take an unplayable lie in a sand bunker and choose one of the first two options, you have to drop your ball in the bunker. (Sorry!)

7. **"Can't I just pick up that short 'gimme' putt and say it's good?"** You can, but it calls for a one-stroke penalty. To avoid being disqualified, take your ball back to where it was and hole it out (count all strokes, plus the one-stroke penalty).

8. **"I'm going to move my ball just a few inches. The grass is 'greener' (and shorter) there!"** Don't listen to that little voice in your head! Anytime you lift, move, or touch a ball that's in play, it's a one-stroke penalty (unless the rules say it's okay). Replace your ball and keep going.

club to the sand before I swing?"
That's right. It's a two-stroke
penalty if you "ground" your club
in a sand bunker or water hazard
area *before* taking your swing.
Add two strokes to your score (if
necessary, recreate the original
lie). In fact, when your ball's in a

sand bunker or water hazard, make sure you don't touch the
water or ground with your hand or club before the swing.
(A pro recently got a two-stroke penalty when his club
happened to touch the water before his swing!)

10. **"My friend said I can't move a pinecone away from my
ball that's in a sand trap. Is this correct?"** Your friend is
right. It's a two-stroke penalty if you move loose impediments (leaves, stones, twigs, pinecones) away from your ball
when you're in a sand bunker or water hazard. Outside a
hazard it's no problem.

> **◆ QUICK TIP ◆**
>
> If your first shot from a bunker doesn't come out, be careful not
> to touch the sand with your club after the shot, otherwise you'll
> be penalized two strokes for grounding your club. Some players
> get upset when their first shot doesn't come out, smack their
> club into the sand, and then really get mad when a two-stroke
> penalty is tacked on!

11. **"I like to step behind my ball when it's in the rough. It gives me a better lie."** Think again! If you move, press down, or break any vegetation that's *growing* near or around your ball, it's a two-stroke penalty. Ditto if you press your clubhead down into the turf behind your ball to im-

prove its lie. Exception: It's fine to step behind your ball before you hit your first shot from the tee box.

12. **"My friend's putt just hit the flagstick. Is this a problem?"** If a putt from the green hits the flagstick or another player's ball, it's a two-stroke penalty. (When your putt hits another player's ball, take his or her ball back to where it was and play your ball where it lies.)

◆▸ QUICK TIP ◂◆

Your ball is "on" the green when any part of the ball touches the green. If it is, you can mark, lift, and clean your ball. Also make sure you have someone tend or take out the flagstick!

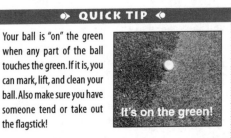

It's on the green!

Always follow golf's first two rules: "Play the course as you find it and play the ball as it lies."

13. "I missed my putt, and then I knocked it back into the hole before it could roll any farther!" Hitting your ball while it's moving is a two-stroke penalty. The same is true if you swing and miss a ball that's moving! Either way it's a problem. Play your ball where it lies.

14. "Is it okay to tap down rough spots on the green between my ball and the hole?" Not usually. The rules say you can't touch your putt line with your club, hand, or foot. (Two penalty strokes.) What can you do? Fix any ball marks and move sand, soil, leaves, or litter away. When you move things away from your ball, make sure you use your hands or a club, and not the visor of your hat, a towel, or anything else.

15. "My shot just flew sideways and hit my golf bag! Oops!" It's a two-stroke penalty if your shot hits you, your bag, or your clubs (after it ricochets off a tree, the lip of a sand trap, or something). What if your shot hits another player or his equipment? No penalty.

16. "I've got to clean that big chunk of mud off my ball!" Don't do it, unless your ball is on the green (or the rules say it's okay). Leave the mud on your ball and keep playing until you reach the green. If you pick it up

and clean it anyway, give yourself a one-stroke penalty. It's also important to remember that you can't clean your ball when seeing if it's unfit for play or when lifting it when it's in the way of another player's ball.

17. **"I was just addressing my ball and it moved. Now what!?"** If you address your ball and touch your club to the turf, and your ball rolls from its original spot, replace your ball and add a penalty stroke to your score.

If you think your ball might move, take your stance but don't touch your club to the ground. If the ball moves, wait until it stops rolling before you begin your swing. Play the ball where it lies. (No penalty.)

18. **"I grabbed a loose tree branch near my ball and my ball moved. Any problem?"** Afraid so. If you move a natural impediment (outside a hazard) such as a tree branch or leaf within one club-length of your ball and your ball moves, you should replace your ball and count a one-

stroke penalty. Exception: If this happens when your ball is on the green, return your ball to its original spot. (No penalty.)

19. **"That guy just pushed his ball into the cup!"** This is an illegal stroke. You can't push or scrape your ball toward the hole at any time. If he wants to do it right, he should replace his ball, count the initial stroke, and add a one-stroke penalty to his score.

20. "Wow, my club just hit my ball twice during the same swing!" Sometimes during a short chip or putt, your club-face will strike the ball more than once. It sounds weird, but it happens. When it does, add two strokes to your score—one for the first stroke and one more as a one-stroke penalty.

21. "How many extra clubs does that guy have in his bag?" The rules say that 14 clubs are all you can carry in your bag (but you can carry more than one type of club as long as the total doesn't exceed 14). (Penalty: Two strokes, with a maximum penalty of four strokes per round.) You also shouldn't share clubs with other players, but you can give away balls and tees.

22. "I think I just hit someone else's ball." Go back and find your own ball, add a two-stroke penalty to your score (but don't count the initial stroke with the wrong ball), and finish the hole. If you finish the hole while playing the wrong ball, it's all over (you're disqualified). Exception: If you were hitting from a hazard, there's no problem as long as you go back and hit your own ball.

23. "After my drive, I like switching to a soft, high-spin ball." Not a good plan! It's a two-stroke penalty if you switch to another ball while you are playing a given hole, unless your ball is unfit (cut, scratched, or out of shape) for play. If you think it is, tell your competitors that you would like to look it over, and then mark and pick it up (just re-member you can't clean your ball as you inspect it).

24. **"I'm going to putt from the fringe; can I move some sand out of the way?"** You can brush sand away that's on the green, but not sand that's sitting on the short grass just off the green. (Two penalty strokes.) The bottom line: Never move sand or soil away from your ball unless it's on the green!

25. **"I like hitting a practice shot or two while I play."** Taking extra practice shots isn't allowed. Add two strokes to your score for each practice shot. Exception: When no one is waiting, you can hit practice putts on the green that you've just played or hit chip shots near the green (but don't practice bunker shots).

26. **I've got to bend those branches out of the way so I can take a full swing."** The rules say you can't move, bend, or break anything growing or fixed, except to fairly take your stance or swing. It's fine to get in close to a tree and take your stance, but you shouldn't bend any branches out of the way so you can take an ideal swing.

27. **"Hey, which club did you use on that shot?"** Sorry, that's confidential! Asking an opponent which club he or she used for a shot *or* telling another player which club you used is a two-stroke penalty. Ditto for asking or telling competitors exactly how far it is to a given target or discussing anything that's not common knowledge or that might give a scoring advantage to a competitor. The USGA believes golf is an in-dividual sport!

Golf Rules Go on Forever!

There's a ton of golf rules, but if you play in local golf tournaments, it's a good idea to know as many of them as you can. To learn as much as possible, study the rules in this lesson and the official USGA rulebook (also published online at usga.org). If you ever get stumped, talk things over with your local PGA club professional.

To finish up this lesson, here are a few more examples:

1. Your partner or caddie can suggest an aim line before you putt, but as this is talked about, no one should touch any part of the green. When you take the stroke, make sure your partner or caddie stands away so they're not behind or along any extension of your putt line.
2. If your ball is in play and you happen to hit it during a practice swing, add a one-stroke penalty to your score. Replace your ball and continue.
3. If you swing at your ball that's in play and miss it, you're supposed to add one stroke to your score for each wiff.
4. If your ball is in casual water within a sand bunker, take a free drop as long as you drop inside the bunker. You can't get out that easy!
5. If your ball is on the green and there's casual water or ground under repair between your ball and the hole, you can move your ball so you have a clear path to the hole. Just make sure you place the ball on the green, no nearer the hole. (No penalty.) If your ball is off the green and there's casual water or ground under repair on the green, play your ball as it lies.

6. You can fix any ball mark on the green, at any time. But don't fix a ball mark that's just off the green until *after* you've hit your shot (or putt).

7. Your ball is "out" only when all of it is on or across the out of bounds line or boundary. If any part of the ball is in bounds, then it's "in."

8. In a water hazard, don't touch the water or the ground with your hand or club before the swing. (Two penalty strokes.) But it is okay for your club to gently touch the long grass surrounding the ball. Exception: You can ground your club if your ball stops on a bridge.

9. If your ball (at rest) is moved by another player or by another ball, take it back to where it was and continue. (No penalty.) However, if your ball (at rest) is moved by a sudden gust of wind, play it as it lies.

10. If your ball rolls as you pick up a rake or hose (a movable obstruction), return your ball to where it was and continue. (No penalty.)

moving, take it back to its original spot and replay your shot. (No penalty.)

12. Don't move dew or frost away from your ball even if it's in the way. Snow and natural ice (other than frost) are either casual water or a loose impediment (you decide what's best).

13. When hitting a shot in the rain or directly into the sun, don't ask someone to hold an umbrella over you or shield the sun from your view. (Two penalty strokes.)

14. If your ball is plugged in the rough or in a bunker, play the ball as it lies or apply the "unplayable lie" rule. If your ball is plugged in grass the length of the fairway or shorter, you can pick it up, clean it, drop it as close as possible to where it was, and continue. (No penalty.)

15. If a stationary bug is on your ball (and you are not in a hazard), you can remove the bug with your fingers. (No penalty.)

16. If your ball flies into an electrical wire or power pole, replay your shot even if the deflection gives you a lucky bounce.

17. On the day of a tournament, don't practice playing any hole or putt on any green. (Penalty: disqualification.) Where can you practice? On any practice range or practice green.

18. When you putt, keep both feet on only one side of the ball (without either foot touching your putt line). This means you can't putt while standing

behind the ball, facing the cup, or setting one foot on either side of the ball.

19. What if my ball's hanging on the edge of the cup? Walk to the cup at a normal pace and wait no more than 10 seconds for the ball to drop. If it doesn't, hole your ball and count the stroke.

20. It's fine to stand out of bounds and hit your ball that's still in bounds. You can also stand outside a tee box and hit a ball that's inside it.

21. To see if a ball is really yours (when it's not in a hazard): Tell your competitions what you plan to do, mark your ball before you touch it, and then pick it up and see if it's yours. If a ball is in a hazard, play it as it lies (the rules say you can't touch it).

22. You can take a free drop from piled grass clippings (to be moved at a later time), but not from abandoned clippings unless they're marked as ground under repair.

23. If you hit your ball into the fairway and you can't tell whether it's yours, the ball is lost (stroke and distance penalty)! This happens when two players hit into the same area and both balls have the same brand name and ball number. How's it prevented? Use an indelible pen and put a unique mark on the ball before you play.

into play, you've got to play that ball (even if you find the original one). Exception: When you hit a provisional ball.

25. You can hold the flagstick in one hand and putt with the other as long as your ball doesn't hit the flagstick and you don't use the flagstick as a crutch to support your body in any way.

26. Don't go in cahoots with another player. You'll be disqualified if there's been a rule violation and both of you agree to overlook it!

27. If you write down a wrong score anywhere on your scorecard (whether it helps you or not) and then sign the card, you'll be disqualified.

Exceptions to the Rules: The USGA allows local committees, running a golf course or a competition, to establish "Local Rules" that override some of the official Rules of Golf. Local Rules, often listed on the course's scorecard or given out on a "Rules Sheet" at the beginning of a tournament, may allow you to: • Play with more than 14 clubs. • Take free relief for an embedded ball anywhere on the course unless you're in a hazard. • Move leaves or loose stones away from your ball when it is in a bunker. • Take free relief from certain manmade obstructions (a distance marker along your line of play). • Play "Winter Rules" (to improve your ball's lie unless you're in a hazard).

> **JUST FOR FUN**
>
> "Golf is the hardest game in the world to play, and the easiest to cheat at."
>
> —Dave Hill

Take-Home Assignment: If you'd like to learn more, go to the USGA website at usga.org (click on the rules section) and read up on the hundreds of examples and scenarios covering every possible rule violation.

Common Goof-ups!

When you play . . .

○ Don't get in the habit of taking mulligans.

○ Never tee your ball ahead of the tee markers.

○ Don't bump your ball to a better spot. Play it as it lies!

○ If you think your ball may be lost or out of bounds, don't forget to hit a provisional shot before you go and look for your original ball.

○ If your ball goes into a water hazard, you can choose from several options. One is to go back behind the hazard as far as you would like, keeping the point at which your original ball last crossed the hazard line between your drop point and the flagstick. But don't misinterpret this! Many players mistakenly go back along their ball's "line of flight" and drop in the safe fairway, which may not keep these three points (the drop point, the place where the ball last crossed the hazard line, and the flagstick) in a straight line.

○ When you're in a hazard, don't touch your hand or club to the water or ground *before* taking your stroke.

○ Don't move a loose leaf, stone, twig, or pinecone away from your ball when it's in a hazard. On the other hand, you can move manmade objects (a paper cup, cigarette butt, or rake) away from your ball at any time.

○ When you're putting on the green, never let your ball roll into the flagstick (or another player's ball).

Recap

● You need to know how to drop your ball back into play when it gets into trouble.

● You can take a free drop from eight different places.

● It's a one-stroke penalty if you . . .

  ▶ hit your ball out of bounds (count the original stroke, plus add a one-stroke penalty to your score).

  ▶ lose your ball (count the original stroke, plus add a one-stroke penalty to your score).

  ▶ hit your ball into a water hazard (count the original stroke, plus add a one-stroke penalty to your score).

  ▶ drop your ball away from a lie that's not playable.

  ▶ pick up a short putt (but then replace your ball and hole it).

  ▶ touch or pick up your ball when it's in play (unless allowed by the rules).

  ▶ clean mud from your ball (unless allowed by the rules).

  ▶ ground your club and, as a result, your ball moves.

  ▶ move a leaf or twig (loose natural impediments) away from your ball and as a result, your ball moves.

- use an illegal putting stroke (count the original stroke, plus add a one-stroke penalty to your score).
- hit your ball more than once during the same swing (count the original stroke, plus add a one-stroke penalty to your score).

● It's a two-stroke penalty if you . . .

- hit your tee shot from in front of the tee markers. (Hit again from inside the box. Don't count the first stroke. Add a two-stroke penalty to your score.)
- touch your club to the ground before hitting from a sand or water hazard.
- move a pinecone or twig (natural impediments) away from your ball when you're in a hazard.
- move, press down, or break any vegetation that's *growing* near or around your ball.
- miss a short putt and then hit your ball while it's still rolling (count the original stroke, plus add a two-stroke penalty to your score).
- touch the green anywhere along your putt line (unless allowed by the rules).
- stroke your ball and then somehow it hits you, your club, or your bag (count the original stroke, plus add a two-stroke penalty to your score).
- carry too many clubs (more than 14).
- hit the wrong ball. (After you find your original ball, don't count the stroke with the wrong ball; add a two-stroke penalty to your score and continue play.)

your original ball is still in good shape).

- ask your competitor which club he or she used on a shot.
- tell your competitor which club you used on a shot.
- use another competitor's club on any hole.
- hit the flagstick (or another player's ball) when you're playing from the green (count the stroke, plus add a two-stroke penalty to your score).
- brush sand or soil away from your ball (when you're playing from off the green).

● You'll be disqualified if you . . .

- don't hole your ball on any green.
- play any hole or putt on any regulation green as a way to "check out" the course on the day of a tournament.
- finish a hole while playing with the wrong ball.
- agree with another player to overlook a rule violation.
- sign an incorrect scorecard.

18

WRAP-UP

Track Your Progress

Use these logs to see your improvement.

Spice Things Up—Play a Game!

Play a game to make your golf fun and competitive.

Heads Up!

There's always more to learn!

The Skinny on Grips, Shafts, and Clubheads

See what beginning and seasoned players carry in their bag.

Golf Partners

Keep an up-to-date list of all the people you like to play golf with.

1. **Distance Check.** Go to a practice range with distance markers and hit at least 10 balls with each club. Write down your average distance (in yards) of each club using a full swing. Every month or so, do this activity again and record your progress.

DISTANCE LOG									
Date									
Sand wedge									
Lob wedge									
Pitching wedge									
9-iron									
8-iron									
7-iron									
6-iron									
5-iron									
4-iron									
3-iron									
5-wood									
3-wood									
1-wood									

2.   **Golf Check.** Keep track of your golf scores, greens hit in regulation,* and total putts as you play.

SCORING LOG							
Date							
Golf course 9-hole yardage							
Golf course 9-hole par							
9-hole score							
Strokes over (or under) par							
Greens hit in regulation							
Number of total putts							

---

*To hit a green in regulation means to hit your ball onto a 3-par green in one shot, a 4-par green in two shots, and a 5-par green in three shots.

Spice Things Up—Play a Game!

Best ball. Two players on the same team play their own ball the entire round. The lowest score for each hole counts as the team's score. The team with the lowest score at the end of play wins the match.

Scramble. Two to four players all hit from the same place. They then choose the shot with the best-placed ball, and everyone moves to that spot. Each player hits another ball from that point, and again everyone moves up to the best-placed shot. This continues until someone holes a putt. The best shots are added up and this equals the team's hole score. At the end of the round, the team with the lowest total score wins the match.

Nassau. Players on two opposing teams compete head-to-head. One point is earned for the best front 9, one point for the best back 9, and one point for the best overall round of 18 holes. The player or team that earns the most total points wins the match.

Play for points. Each player (or team) earns a point on each hole when he or she:

- Hits the longest drive *in* the fairway (1 point)
- Hits the first ball onto the green (1 point)
- Hits the closest shot to pin from off the green (1 point)
- Sinks the longest putt (1 point)
- Gets the lowest score on the hole (1 point)

Note: Take a point away for any three putt (minus 1 point)

At the end of the round, the player or team that earns the most points wins the match.

Skins. Two to four players try to win a "skin" on each hole by achieving the best or lowest score. In the event of a tie, the skin is carried over or added to the next hole. How much is each skin worth? The players decide. The value can stay the same or increase as the round progresses. The player with the most skins at the end of the round wins the match.

Wolf. A foursome is needed to play this game. On each hole, a different player takes a turn as the "Wolf." After everyone has hit their tee shots, the designated Wolf either: (a) chooses one partner OR (b) plays alone as the "Lone Wolf" against the other three players.

You earn points on each hole depending on how the teams are organized.

- With two players on each team:

  ▶ If the Wolf's team score is lower (by adding each player's score together), both players on the Wolf's team earn *two* points.

  ▶ If the other team's combined score beats the Wolf's team, each player on the other team earns *three* points.

- With a Lone Wolf playing against the other three players:

  ▶ If the Lone Wolf's score (multiplied by 2) is lower than the two *best* scores of the other team added together, the Lone Wolf earns *four* points.

  ▶ If the two best scores of the other team added together is lower than the Lone Wolf's score (multiplied by 2), each player on the other team earns *five* points.

The winner is the player who earns the most points by the end of the match.

Heads Up!

Here's a listing of major golf tournaments to watch each year:

MAJOR CHAMPIONSHIPS		
PGA Tour (men's)	**LPGA Tour (ladies)**	**Champions Tour (men's, 50 and older)**
The Masters early April masters.org	**Nabisco Championship** late March lpga.com	**The Tradition** late April
U.S. Open mid-June usopen.com	**LPGA Championship** early June lpga.com	**Senior PGA Championship** early June pga.com
British Open mid-July opengolf.com	**U.S. Women's Open** early July lpga.com	**U.S. Senior Open** late June usga.org
PGA mid-August pga.com	**Women's British Open** early August lpga.com	**Senior Players Championship** mid-July

Want to learn more about the game? Choose from the following books, magazines, and websites:

Books

Hogan, Ben, 1957. *Five Lessons—The Modern Fundamentals of Golf.* New York: Simon & Schuster.

Leadbetter, David, with John Huggan. 1990. *The Golf Swing.* New York: Penguin Books.

Penick, Harvey, with Bud Shrake. 1992. *Harvey Penick's Little Red Book.* New York: Simon & Schuster.

The United States Golf Association. *The Rules of Golf 2002–03.* Far Hills, New Jersey: USGA.

Watson, Tom, with Frank Hannigan. 1996. *The New Rules of Golf.* New York: Random House.

Magazines

Golf Magazine. To subscribe call: 800-876-7726.

Golf Digest. To subscribe call: 800-PAR-GOLF.

Websites

golfonline.com

usga.org

pga.com

lpga.com

Here's the scoop on golf clubs:

Grips

The grips on your clubs should feel good and fit the size of your hands. Most players go with a standard grip size, but if your hands are on the small or large side, you may need a different grip—one that's a bit smaller or larger than normal. Ask a local golf shop expert for help if you're not sure what you need.

When your grips become slippery and worn out, take your clubs to a golf shop repair center and have the grips replaced. (It's not very expensive.) If you play regularly, plan to regrip your clubs about every year or so.

Note: Some players learn how to regrip their own clubs since it's easy to do and lowers the cost.

Shafts

Most shafts are made of either graphite or steel. A club with a graphite shaft usually produces a bit more clubhead speed than one with a steel shaft, so it's a popular choice for the 1-wood or driver.

Most players use steel shafts on all of their other clubs, but some beginners like graphite shafts on all of their woods and irons because of a slight yardage advantage.

How much your clubshaft flexes or bends during the downswing has a big effect on the length, trajectory, and accuracy of your shots. Get the wrong shaft flex and the game is a lot harder. For instance, if your shaft is too stiff (for your swing), the clubhead will lag behind the hands as it comes in to the ball, causing your shot to fly high and off to the right. On the flipside, if your shaft is too whippy your clubhead will jump ahead of your hands, causing your shot to fly low and off to the left.

Of course, the faster you swing, the stiffer your shaft needs to be. For example, the shaft you choose depends on how far you hit an average drive:

> < 180 yards = Ladies or Senior Flex
> 180–210 yards = Flexible (A-Flex)
> 210–240 yards = Regular or Firm Flex
> 240–280 yards = Stiff Flex
> > 280 yards = Extra-Stiff Flex

The trajectory of your shots is also influenced by how much the shaft twists ("torque") and where it bends on the downswing (the "kick point"). With everything else the same, a shaft with less torque (less twisting) and a higher kick point creates a lower trajectory shot, while more torque and a lower kick point creates a higher trajectory shot. (Surprisingly, the shaft's torque and kick point have more effect on the shot's height than on its direction.)

Before you make your final decision on which shaft to use, talk things over with a golf shop expert and hit some practice balls with different shafts to see how they feel.

Irons

Over the past 20 years, irons have changed a lot—mostly to help the beginning player. What's the biggest improvement? The creation of perimeter-weighted "cavity-back" or "casted" irons. These irons look like the name suggests—

with a cavity hollowed out of the backside of the clubhead. The extra weight is then redistributed around the perimeter of the clubhead. This makes the sweet-spot area (the part of the clubface that allows for the best hit) larger so that even when the ball is hit near the toe or heel of the clubface, you can still enjoy a decent shot.

Surprisingly, not every golfer plays with cavity-back irons. Some advanced players like traditional or classic "blade" irons (also called "forged" or "muscle-back" irons) instead. These irons give a crisper "feel" when the ball is hit on the sweet spot, which boosts confidence. They are also better at shaping a shot around a tree or into a tight pin position.

But blades are not a good idea for beginners. The sweet spot is so small (about the size of a dime) that there is much less margin for error. If the ball is hit just a little off-center (closer to the toe or to the heel), the shot will always turn out bad! Cavity-back irons are a much better choice for beginning players.

Recently, club makers have come up with a hybrid-type iron that blends the feel of a blade with the forgiveness of a cavity-back. But so far these clubs aren't forgiving enough for beginning players.

Woods

Traditional wooden-headed woods are a thing of the past. Now woods are made from steel, graphite, or titanium. Like cavity-back irons, metal woods are perimeter-weighted, very forgiving, and easy to hit with. Plus, metal woods drive the ball farther than traditional woods. Because of this, players of all skill levels use metal woods.

Clubhead Size

Oversized heads (on irons or woods) have a bigger sweet spot than regular-sized heads, so they're easier to hit with and a better choice for beginners. Seasoned players, on the other hand, go with whichever clubhead looks good, feels right, and gives them the best results.

A Few More Things to Consider

Club Weight

When you swing any club, it shouldn't feel too heavy or too light. To accommodate players of different strength levels, a wide variety of swingweights (which basically means how heavy the club feels during the swing) are available, ranging from C-7 to D-5, while most women's clubs range from C-2 to D-0.

Clubhead Lie Angle

When an iron swings into the ball and cuts into the turf, the bottom or sole of the club should be level with the ground. This means that one end of the sole will not dig in deeper than the other; the divot will be flat. To make this possible, golf club manufacturers produce irons with flat, standard, and upright lie angles (the angle between the shaft and the bottom of the clubhead).

JUST FOR FUN

"My worst day on the golf course still beats my best day at the office."

—John Hallisey

Usually, a standard lie angle works for medium-height players (5'8" to 6'), a 1-degree flat lie works for shorter players (5'5" to 5'8"), and a 1-degree upright lie works for taller players (6' to 6'2").

To find the lie angle that's right for you, get some expert advice, hit some practice balls, and go with the club that produces the flattest divot and the straightest shot. (*Note:* Woods usually come with a standard lie angle since no divot is taken.)

Club Length

Your clubs should be long enough so that you can take a comfortable stance and not feel overly extended or cramped in any way. If your height is between 5'8" to 6'2", a *standard* shaft length will probably work (remember men's clubs are about an inch longer than women's). If you are shorter or taller than this, you may need to have custom clubs built to fit your height.

Putters

Putters come in a variety of shapes and sizes, so you will need to experiment to find the putter that works best for you. Differences in the grip, shaft length, and putter-head design complicate the deci-

sion. A good putter usually costs from $75 to $120 but can be as expensive as $250 or more. What's interesting is that the price of the putter has very little to do with how well you will putt. What really counts is how well you can stroke the ball with a perfectly squared putterface and just the right amount of force!

Number of Clubs

A half-set works well for beginners, which includes two metal woods, four cavity-back irons (a 4-, 6-, 8-, and pitching wedge), and a putter. Some beginners go with a 3- and 5-wood instead of a 1- and 3-wood since the 1-wood is harder to hit with.

Advanced players use a full set of 14 clubs, which includes three metal woods (a 1-, 3-, and 5-wood), seven blade or cavity-back irons (a 3-, 4-, 5-, 6-, 7-, 8-, and 9-iron), a pitching wedge, a lob wedge, a sand wedge, and a putter. Many advanced players also own other clubs, such as a 1-iron, a 2-iron, and several lob wedges, that they switch in and out of their bag depending on what works best for the course they are about to play.

GOLF PARTNERS

NAME	PHONE	BEST TIME TO PLAY

Credits

Ace: A hole-in-one.

Address: A golfer's stance and posture before taking a swing.

Aim line: An imaginary line running from your ball to the target; also called the target line.

Approach: A shot played to the putting green.

Back nine: The second 9 holes of an 18-hole course; also called the back side.

Birdie: A score of one stroke less than par on a hole.

Bogie: A score of one stroke above par on a hole.

Bunker: A hazard near a green or fairway where the turf has been removed and replaced with sand; also called a sand trap.

Casual water: Standing water on the course that's not inside a water hazard; a puddle from a rainstorm or sprinkler.

Chip: A low shot from near the green that rolls most of the way to the hole; also called a bump-and-run.

Closed clubface: When the clubface points to the left (the toe of the clubface leads the heel) as the ball is hit; makes the shot curve to the left.

Closed stance: A stance with the left foot closer to the aim line than the right.

Divot: The grass and soil cut from the turf when a swing is taken.

Dogleg: When a hole bends sharply to the right or to the left.

Double bogie: A score of two strokes above par on a hole.

Double eagle: A score of three strokes less than par on a 5-par hole; also called an albatross.

Draw: A shot that curves *slightly* to the left.

Drive: The first shot taken on par-4 and par-5 holes.

Driver: The number-1 wood.

Drop: The way you put your ball back in play; it may or may not involve a penalty.

Eagle: A score of two strokes less than par on a hole.

Executive course: A short golf course with mostly par threes, perfect for beginning golfers.

Fade: A shot that curves *slightly* to the right.

Fairway: The safe, short grass area between the tee-ing area and the green.

Fat shot: Hitting the turf an inch or two behind the ball; also called chunking it.

Flagstick: A long, narrow fiberglass pole with a flag on the top; shows where the cup is located on the green; also called the pin.

Fore!: A loud warning call to anyone in danger of being hit by a golf ball.

Foursome: A group of four golfers playing together.

Fringe: The short grass surrounding the green; also called the apron or collar.

Front nine: The first 9 holes of an 18-hole course; also called the front side.

Green fee: The cost to play 9 or 18 holes.

Handicap: Refers to a player's skill level; roughly equals the number of strokes over par a player shoots on 18 holes.

Hazard: A bunker or water hazard from which a free drop is not allowed.

play first from the tee (when you win a coin toss on the first hole or have the lowest score on a previous hole).

Hook: A shot that curves to the left.

Intermediate target: A spot just in front of your ball (on your aim line) that helps you line up your shot accurately.

LPGA: Ladies Professional Golf Association.

Lateral water hazard: A lake or river running alongside the hole, marked with red stakes or a red line.

Loose impediments: A natural object like a stone, leaf, pinecone, or twig that is not growing or attached to the ground.

Magic move: To begin the downswing with your hips and legs, and not your arms or shoulders; a key ingredient to a powerful swing.

Match play: A hole-by-hole competition. The player who wins the most individual holes (with the lowest score on a given hole) wins the match.

Mulligan: To hit an extra ball when your first shot wasn't good enough (not allowed by the USGA rules of golf).

Obstruction: A manmade object like a rake, litter, hose, fence, or stake that is not a part of the course; may be movable or immovable.

Open clubface: When the clubface points to the right (the heel of the clubface leads the toe) as the ball is hit; makes the shot curve to the right.

Open stance: A stance with the right foot closer to the target line than the left; often used on short approach shots.

Out of bounds: The area where play is not allowed, marked with white stakes, a white line, or a fence.

PGA: Professional Golfer's Association.

Par: The number of strokes a scratch golfer takes to complete a hole.

Parallel-left: To align your stance line parallel to your aim line; this puts your stance line left (and parallel) of your aim line.

Penalty strokes: The stroke(s) added to your score when you violate a rule.

Pitch: An approach shot that flies most of the way to the hole and then rolls a short distance.

Playing through: To allow a faster group to play ahead of a slower one.

Practice range: An area to practice golf shots; also called a driving range.

Provisional ball: To hit an extra ball when you believe your original ball is lost or out of play (a practice encouraged by the USGA to save time).

Pull: A shot that flies straight but goes to the left of the target.

Push: A shot that flies straight but goes to the right of the target.

Putt: A stroke made on the green with a putter.

Relief: To move your ball away from trouble without a penalty; also called a free drop.

Rough: Long grass or vegetation that lines the edges of the fairway.

Sand save or "sandy": To take one shot from a green-side bunker and then one putt to hole your ball.

Scratch golfer: A player whose handicap is zero and is able to shoot an even-par score on 9 or 18 holes.

Shank: To hit the ball on the neck or hosel of the club; makes the ball veer sharply to the right.

Sky: A shot that pops up and flies really high.

Slice: A shot that curves to the right.

Square clubface: When the clubface faces the target as the ball is hit; produces a straight shot.

Square stance: A stance with both feet the same distance from the target line; used on mid-range and long shots.

Stance line: An imaginary line, running across the toes, knees, hips, or shoulders, that's exactly parallel and left of the aim line.

Stroke play (medal play): A competition where the winner shoots the lowest total score on 9 or more holes.

Teeing area: The area between the tee markers from which you can tee your ball at the beginning of each hole; also called a tee box.

Tee-time: A reservation to play a round of golf at a specified time.

Tending the flag: To hold the flagstick while another player putts and then to remove the flagstick before the ball reaches the hole.

Top: A shot that flies low or rolls along the ground; also called a thin or skulled shot.

Up and down: To hit a chip or pitch from just off the green, and then one putt to hole your ball.

Waggle: To slowly move the clubhead back and forth behind the ball just before the swing; helps the player relax and loosen up.

Water hazard: A lake or stream situated between the teeing area and the green, marked with yellow stakes or a yellow line.

Index